THE
POLITICS
OF
SOUTH AFRICA

Henry Allan Fagan (1889–1963)

THE
POLITICS
OF
SOUTH AFRICA

*Democracy
and Racial Diversity*

HOWARD BROTZ

OXFORD LONDON NEW YORK
OXFORD UNIVERSITY PRESS
1977

Oxford University Press, Walton Street, Oxford OX2 6DP

OXFORD LONDON GLASGOW NEW YORK
TORONTO MELBOURNE WELLINGTON CAPE TOWN
IBADAN NAIROBI DAR ES SALAAM LUSAKA ADDIS ABABA
KUALA LUMPUR SINGAPORE JAKARTA HONG KONG TOKYO
DELHI BOMBAY CALCUTTA MADRAS KARACHI

ISBN 0 19 215671 3

© *Howard Brotz* 1977

British Library Cataloguing in Publication Data

Brotz, Howard Merwin
     The Politics of South Africa : democracy and
     racial diversity.
     Index
     ISBN 0–19–215671–3
     1. Title
     320.9′68′05   JQ1924
     South Africa – Politics and government – 1909 –

*Printed in Great Britain
by Ebenezer Baylis and Son Ltd,
The Trinity Press, Worcester, and London*

In Memoriam

MIRIAM BROTZ
BETTY LUNN

Preface

This book began as a study of the impact of industrialization upon racial policy in contemporary South Africa. To make sense out of this policy I was compelled to investigate the idea which is at the core of apartheid; namely, that the Blacks in the towns must be either defined as 'guest-workers', or else enfranchised on a common electoral roll. Such an historical inquiry was necessary because the origins of this idea had become obscured by the rhetoric both defending and attacking apartheid. In the course of this inquiry I encountered a discussion of what constitutional democracy demands in South Africa, which had taken issue with the above idea even before the Nationalists came into power in 1948. Inasmuch as the rhetoric since then seems to be a running away from that question, it may be of some interest to restore this pristine discussion, with its freedom from partisan prejudices and moral indignation. It seems to have been forgotten. In fact it hangs like a ghost over the politics of South Africa.

I should like to thank the numerous individuals from whom I have learned something about South Africa, all of whom, over the course of thirteen years of recurrent study, it would be impossible to acknowledge by name. Of those whom I am going to mention I must thank first Professor Gwendolen Carter for getting me interested in South Africa, and for her great help in getting this study under way. In South Africa itself I should like to thank for their special and repeated help M. G. Buthelezi, S. P. Cilliers, J. Coetzee, Moira Farmer, R. Fredman, R. J. Friedland, Robin Fryde, P. H. Ganswyk, Harry Goldberg, Teresa and Charles Graham, Freda La Grange, O. S. Graupner, Lulu Grobbelaar, Ellen Hellman, W. Kgware, Jan Kirstein, Willem Kleynhans, S. J. J. Lesolang, Henry Lever, Julius Lewin, David and Betty Lunn, A. H. I. Mahomedy, E. G. Malherbe, Ismail Mayet, Solly Melzer, H. W. van der Merwe, F. N. Mncube, M. T. Moerane, S. Motsuenyane, Armstrong Mphahlele, Schalk Pienaar, Collins and Mary Jane

Ramusi, Harry Rajak, R. E. van der Ross, Gus Saron, J. H. Serfontein, Theodore Seroke, Raymond Silberbauer, Joan Verster, F. J. van Wyk, and David Zeffert.

The officials of the Non-European Affairs Department of the city of Johannesburg, and of the Ministry of Information in Pretoria, Johannesburg, Durban, Cape Town, and King Williamstown were extremely helpful in enabling me to see whatever I wanted. In particular, I should like to acknowledge the kind assistance given me by Mr. W. Davies, Dr. E. J. Jammine, and the late Mr. C. Prinsloo.

I should like to acknowledge with thanks the financial support given me over the course of this study by Smith College, the Ford Foundation's African–Asian Studies Program in the Connecticut Valley, the Earhart Foundation, and the Canada Council. The Comparative Industrial Societies Program of McMaster University has helped to defray the costs of preparing the manuscript.

I should like to thank Juta & Company and the family of the late H. A. Fagan for permission to quote from his writings. I should particularly like to thank Mrs. Q. Fagan for permission to reproduce as a frontispiece the photograph of her late husband from her book *Henry Allan Fagan 1889–1963* (Cape Town, 1975).

Finally I should like to express my very great indebtedness to Mr. Ian Elgie, now of the University of Zambia, for his care and skill in translating, wherever possible, opinion into fact. He prepared all the tables and maps, and was a great help throughout the course of this study.

Contents

Tables

Maps

I

Politics

Introduction

What is undeniably the most massive political fact in the history of South Africa since the South African War is the rise to political supremacy of Afrikaner nationalism, which, as the saying goes, 'regained at the ballot box what it lost on the battlefield'. Since 1948 the National Party, which emerged and took power as the party of the Afrikaner *volk* (people), has been continuously in office. What is more, it increased its strength in every general election until that of 1970, and then recovered its momentum in the 1974 election. It is understandable that many people, facing what seems to be a government that can never be voted out of office, have looked upon the political course of Afrikaner nationalism as something inevitable that could not have been stopped. There has been much sober thought in South Africa on behalf of this view, not to mention the many rhetorical statements of either apologia or despair. In this chapter I shall present an alternative thesis. This is that the success of Afrikaner nationalism, when seen sociologically from the perspective of the actors in the situation *before the fact*, not only was not inevitable but was in fact a goal derided as a utopian dream by established opinion. Hence, its realization from within the perspective of the actors themselves could at best be the outcome of a long struggle against great odds; a struggle, however, in which chance played into the hands of the tenacious. The preference for the one thesis as against the other is far from being a matter of academic antiquarianism. To liberate the history of Afrikaner nationalism from the extraneous postulate of 'historical inevitability' means to confront not the strength but rather the weakness of the Nationalists' support in public opinion during the first phase of their regime. With this initial weakness in view, we must then begin to ask what made it so and why it has changed. While the answers to these questions

Table 1
Strength of political parties after general elections, 1910–74 (by seats)

Party	1910	1915	1920	1921	1924	1929	1933	1938[b]	1943	1948	1953[a]	1958	1961	1966	1970	1974
National	—	27	44	45	63	78	75	27	43	70 ↗	94	103	105	126	117	123
Afrikaner	—	—	—	—	—	—	—	—	—	9	—	—	—	—	—	—
United	68	—	—	—	—	—	—	111 ↗	89	65	57	53	49	39	47	41
South African	—	54	41 ↗	79	52	61	61 ↗	—	—	—	—	—	—	—	—	—
Unionist	37	39	25	—	—	—	—	—	—	—	—	—	—	—	—	—
Labour	3	4	21	9	18	8	4	3	9	6	5	—	—	—	—	—
Dominion	—	—	—	—	—	—	—	8	7	—	—	—	—	—	—	—
Progressive	—	—	—	—	—	—	—	—	—	—	—	—	1	1	1	6
National Union	—	—	—	—	—	—	—	—	—	—	—	—	1	—	—	—
Independents & vacant seats	13	6	3	1	2	1	10	1	2	—	—	—	—	—	1	1[c]
Native Representatives	—	—	—	—	—	—	—	3	3	3	3	3	—	—	1	—
Coloureds' Representatives	—	—	—	—	—	—	—	—	—	—	—	4	4	—	—	—
Total seats:	121	130	134	134	135	148	150	153	153	153	159	163	160	166	166	171

Sources: Kenneth A. Heard, *General Elections in South Africa 1943–1970*, Oxford University Press, London, 1974, xii, 21, 41, 59, 83, 141, 171; *Star*, 25 April 1974.

Notes: (a) From 1953 the 6 seats for the South West African representatives are included.

(b) These were Purified Nationalists who had refused to enter into the fusion of 1934. All later growth in the N.P. is an expansion of this party. It restyled itself the Herenigde [Re-united] Nasionale Party in 1940, and in 1951 returned to the old name of the National Party.

(c) This was a vacant seat in Pinelands, captured by the Progressives from the U.P. in a subsequent by-election.

do not explain everything, they are, none the less, indispensable elements for understanding the politics of South Africa, then and now.

Ethnic fission and fusion: the dynamics of party realignment

South African political history, since the formation of the Union in 1910, presents the following cycle. An Afrikaner prime minister is in power, seeking to pursue a moderate course between the extreme claims of British supremacy on the one hand and a return to republican independence on the other. He seeks his support among the moderates of both language groups who can be united on the principle of 'South Africanism'. This is the South African equivalent of Canadian 'federalism', *vis-à-vis* provincial autonomy in general, but that of Quebec in particular. Afrikaner nationalism, the South African counterpart to Quebec 'separatism', then emerges politically as an extreme assertion of ethnic interests. It takes the form of a break with the regnant prime minister and his party on the grounds that the interests of the Afrikaner people are being injured, neglected, or compromised. The outstanding grievances are such that the leadership of the extreme group can easily make a case with enough of its following to become the parliamentary opposition. In the course of time the extreme takes power. In doing this, the extreme, now the government, is compelled or induced to move towards the centre. This means, first and foremost, making a rapprochement with English-speaking voters.* As the government becomes a centre in this respect, it then precipitates the rise of a new extreme of Afrikaner nationalism, which starts the cycle again. The new extreme splits from its parent and behaves very much as the latter did when it first arose.

This process of ethnic fission has occurred three times. The first was in 1913 when Hertzog broke with Botha and Smuts to form the National Party. The second was in 1934 when Dr. Malan, refusing to follow Hertzog into the fusion with Smuts, broke with Hertzog to form the 'Purified' National Party. And the third was in 1969 when Dr. Albert Hertzog, a few years after Dr. Verwoerd appointed two English-speakers to his cabinet and began to woo the English vote, broke with the National Party to form the Herstigte [Re-established] Nasionale Party. In the first two cases the extreme came to power. The results of the 1974 election, however, indicate that the Herstigtes, deviating from the careers of their predecessors, have been contained as

* Often referred to in this book as 'the English'.

a fringe, for in two successive general elections they have not been able to elect a single member of parliament.

It would appear that the old cycle is not going to repeat itself. The fact that the Nationalist Government has been able to put down this challenge from the extreme right may mean no more than that the really crucial struggle, between (to use South African terminology) *verligte* and *verkrampte*,* is yet to come, that is, within the National Party itself. How the outcome of this will affect the party structure in South Africa, and what implications this has for the settlement of the race problem, are the decisive questions that we must consider. Let us begin by bringing out in sociological relief the essential historical details of this process of fusion and fission. This, as we shall show, is the key to understanding the structure of political power in South Africa, which affects everything else. In this sketch we must show not only the ethnic and class factors that were at work, but also the accidental events which impinged upon the system from outside.

1910–1948: the rise and fall of the first centre coalition

South Africa in the first decades of this century was still experiencing the initial phase of the industrial revolution which had begun before the South African War and had been one of its contributing causes. This revolution started with the discovery, first of diamonds in Kimberley, and then of gold-bearing reefs in the Witwatersrand. This in turn laid the foundations of domestic manufacturing and modern agriculture. It was altogether to transform the character of what had been a backward rural society. Industrialization sounded the death-knell of an easy-going rural economy among both Whites and Blacks, in which domestic herds were valued for status rather than for a market. Such an economy depended for its perpetuation upon inexhaustible supplies of free land; and when this condition no longer obtained, the economy became decrepit and could no longer carry all its population. Industrialization was to draw both the poor-Whites and the tribal Blacks who were displaced from the land, between whom there

---

* These terms, which were coined by Professor W. de Klerk, immediately caught on and became anglicized in South Africa, so I shall use them as English words. Since they are political terms, dictionary definitions may be somewhat misleading. *verligte* literally means enlightened. *verkrampte,* which is not even in the *Tweetalige Woordeboek,* means narrow or cramped. What they actually mean is moderate and extremist. *Verligte* does not mean liberal except, perhaps, in the pre-modern sense of the word, which does not have the connotations of an 'ism'. Nouns formed from these two are *verligtheid* and *verkramptheid*.

were the rawest racial prejudices, into competition in the urban labour market. It ultimately was to make possible a solution of the economic problems of both, enabling both to acquire a higher level of moral and political awareness than they had previously possessed. But, as in parallel situations elsewhere, industrialization did not do this without creating severe dislocations and problems in the short run.

In 1910 the Afrikaners were still a predominantly rural people. In the mining towns that sprang up on the gold reef, capital was English as was skilled labour, the unskilled labour in the mines being provided by migratory Black tribesmen. There was also a number (small, compared with the number in the United States) of Jewish immigrants from Eastern Europe, principally Lithuania, who were shopkeepers and artisans in the towns and *dorps* (villages), and also itinerant pedlars throughout the *platteland*. In the first parliament Botha, the Prime Minister and leader of the South African Party, had his primary base of support in the *platteland*; but he also had the support of moderate English such as, on the highest level, the men in his cabinet who saw eye to eye with him about his 'South Africanism'. In opposition was a purely English party, the Unionist Party, which was the spokesman for the Chamber of Mines and stood for British supremacy. Between the Government and the Opposition was the (English-speaking) Labour Party. This stood for a White-labour policy directed against the mining interests, and held three seats.

The first break in party structure came in 1913 when Hertzog withdrew with his Orange Free State following from the South African Party to form the National Party. Underneath this split were two related issues. The first was the language question, with Hertzog demanding compulsory instruction in both official languages in the schools. The second was the issue of national versus imperial loyalties and interests. Hertzog's primary opponents were the Unionists, the 'jingoes' and/or the mining magnates, against whom he spoke of South Africa as belonging to the *ware* (true) *Afrikaner*. For this he was accused by the English press of provoking 'racialism', a charge which he indignantly denied and which was in fact not true. In the usage of that time Hertzog was always prepared to regard as South Africans or 'Afrikaners' the English in South Africa who put 'South Africa first'. And his 'two-stream' policy fully recognized the cultural rights of the English. None the less, he had become an embarrassment to Botha in his dealings with the English in the Government.[1]

As we shall see, Hertzog's attack against English capital had to be made vocal by English-speaking Labour before it could be freed from ethnic overtones. But in the first 'Programme of Principles' issued by the National Party in 1914 one can see why Hertzog was not yet ready to listen to Labour. This is because at that time he still thought that relief for the displaced *bywoners* (tenant farmers), the poor-Whites who were 'congesting' the towns, lay in their resettlement on the land.[2] Hence, he could condemn the demand for immigration from overseas, as he did in a speech in 1910, as a 'cry of the capitalists'.[3] Evidently he still looked upon the rise of the towns very much as Kruger did, namely, as the workings of a British imperialist plot to plant Babylons full of *uitlanders* (foreigners) who would take over the country. It was only when he saw—and he saw this within a few years—that the destiny of the poor-Whites, who had never been real farmers in any event, lay in their absorption in the urban industrial structure, that he freed himself from this prejudice.

The effect of the split between Hertzog and Botha was to make Botha dependent upon the Unionists, an alliance which would prove incapable of being the basis of a majority coalition. This fact was obscured for a time by the First World War, during which the English closed ranks behind Botha and Smuts. These two generals not only supported the war but suppressed a rebellion for Afrikaner independence led by men who had been their former comrades-in-arms. Hertzog, while he did not support the war, stood aloof from the rebellion, and thus made a distinction between constitutional and violent change which would have a politically significant parallel later on.

When the war ended, Hertzog and Dr. Malan went to Paris to demand the restoration of the independence of the Transvaal and the Orange Free State in accordance with Woodrow Wilson's principle of self-determination. More consequential was the post-war slump. The 1920 election saw a drift away from both the South African Party and the Unionists to the National Party and the Labour Party, which jumped in strength from 4 to 21 seats. Smuts, who had succeeded upon Botha's death in 1919 to the leadership of the South African Party, offered to enter into a coalition with Hertzog. But Hertzog imposed the right of secession from the British Empire as a condition, to which Smuts would not agree. With the South African Party's strength down to 41 seats, Smuts had two choices before him—either to resign as Botha himself had wanted to do in his last year or to merge his party with the Unionists. He chose to do the latter and was returned to power in the general election he called in 1921.

Smuts now had a clear majority, and in fact the strength of the

enlarged South African Party exceeded the combined strength of the
two members of the coalition in the 1920 election. Its weakness, however, did not disappear but was made critical by the Rand Strike of
1922. This strike was triggered by the intention of the mine-owners to
lower the colour bar in order to keep the low-grade mines in operation
during the slump. The strike was infiltrated by Communists who
paraded the slogan, 'Workers of the World, Fight and Unite for a White
South Africa.'[4] When the strike turned into a political revolt, with the
formation of *commandos*, whose first action was to attack Black com-
pounds, it was suppressed by Smuts with armed force. The strike
collapsed. The result of this, however, was to embitter White labour
and to forge a political alliance between Afrikaner nationalism and the
English-speaking Labour Party. When the first moves towards this
coalition became known, Smuts derided it as a kind of chimera. In fact,
underneath it lay a very clear-cut common interest or outlook, namely,
the White-labour policy.

The thesis of Creswell, the leader of the Labour Party, was that the
'big financial view' that he saw as dominant in the South African
Party, preferred the employment of cheap Black labour working on
indentures or contracts to organized White labour.[5] This thesis, with
all its partisan exaggeration, was now more congenial to Hertzog,
given the fact that the numbers of poor-Whites entering the towns had
begun to assume the character of a mass, irreversible influx. The White-
labour policy in South Africa that Creswell had been advocating since
1905 sprang from a similar root to that of the parallel policy in
Australia, as well as of the anti-immigration and in particular the anti-
Oriental policies in Canada and the United States, all of which were
contemporary. This root was the economic fear felt by organized White
labour of unrestricted competition for employment with racial groups
who would work for lower wages. Besides this economic fear there was
also a political one of being swamped, that fused with labour's more
strictly economic concerns. But the latter were powerful in their own
right and were accentuated in an atmosphere in which social Darwinism
still dominated the relations between capital and labour. To be sure
the implementation of this policy in South Africa, unlike the situation
in Australia (but like that in the American South), had a mainly
domestic dimension. This was because the mines had begun operations
on a base of tribal Black labour, at a time when unskilled White labour
had not yet been displaced from the trek-Boer economy. When the
Whites later moved in to work in the mines, they shunned employments performed by Blacks as 'Kaffir work'. As a result the movement

to restrict labour for unskilled poor-Whites as well as for skilled resulted in demands for ceilings on Black employments. But Creswell also sought to discourage Blacks from emigrating to the towns. To this end, for example, he advocated 'the development of the Natives in suitable Native reserves'.[6] Both this and Labour's 'economic national-ism' (the promotion by state assistance of domestic manufacturing) were ideas that were now also congenial to Hertzog.[7] In fact there is not a single idea advocated by the Nationalists the economic root of which is the protection and improvement of the position of White labour, that had not been thought out by the English-speaking Labour Party a decade before Afrikaner nationalism had any interest in it. The reason for this is not that Labour was less liberal or more racialist in the abstract. It is rather that Labour had fully accepted the existence of the urban industrial system at a time when Afrikaner nationalism was still inclined to see it as 'imperialism'.

The only basis of cleavage between the two members of the coalition was the ethnic one, between English and Afrikaner. This concerned the big issue that had blocked the coalition between Hertzog and Smuts in 1921, namely the 'secession bogey'. On this score English Labour's sentiments were no different from those of the Unionists. Creswell, in his letter to Hertzog proposing the terms of the coalition, firmly ruled out any agitation on the part of the Nationalists to 'cut the painter' as a condition of the coalition.[8] Hertzog was evidently prepared to accept as a legitimate claim from the English Labour Party that which he would not accept as such either from the Unionists or still less from another Afrikaner. When the Nationalists agreed to Creswell's terms, the two groups formed an electoral pact not to stand against one another; and in the election of 1924 the 'Pact Government', as it was called, came to power. Hertzog became the Prime Minister with Labour holding the balance.

In the election of 1929, however, the Nationalists were returned to power with a majority in their own right. This was a clear effect of the Pact Government's White-labour policy. Afrikaner workers who had voted for Labour in 1920 and 1924 switched to the Nationalists, who now stood for the same policy. The National Party in 1929 was be-coming what it became much more pointedly after 1948: a party in which urban White labour (now preponderantly Afrikanerized) would be a paramount segment of its electoral support and would acquire a paramount voice in its policies. And in 1929 Afrikaans capital was in its infancy. The effect of the Pact's policy upon the Labour Party, on the other hand, was that it began to die a slow death. It could only expand by going left, and this meant to champion the cause of the unenfranchised and unorganized Blacks. One section of Labour thought this way, which ultimately caused a split in this dwindling party.

By 1933 the world economic crisis was causing the cohesion of Hertzog's support to become eroded. This was because the economic problem in South Africa was a self-inflicted one. The Nationalists' 'anti-imperialism' led them to cling to the gold standard after Britain had left it, which caused unemployment. This then triggered machinations from within the Nationalist ranks to depose Hertzog and replace him by a coalition with Smuts. The outcome of the crisis, however, was that Hertzog, having abandoned the gold standard, himself entered into, first, a coalition with Smuts's South African Party, and then, a year later (1934), a fusion with it to form the United Party. In this Smuts magnanimously agreed to serve as Deputy Prime Minister.

The way for this fusion had been paved by the Statute of Westminster (1931), which, with the Status of the Union Act (1934), satisfied Hertzog's demands about the sovereign independence of South Africa. The fusion was heralded as a milestone in the political history of the Union, bringing together Afrikaners and English in a massive centre party that seemed to put to rest in a decisive manner the bitter memories of the South African War. The status of the United Party as precisely such a centre is shown by both the character and the small size of the two groups which refused to enter this ethnic coalition. The first was the extreme of Afrikaner nationalism, the nineteen (with one exception) Cape members led by Dr. Malan who mistrusted Smuts as the tool of British imperialism. These men constituted themselves as the Purified National Party and became the official opposition. As events were to show, this small party was to grow to take power in 1948 and hold it to the present day. Its counterpart at the time of the fusion was the extreme of the British imperial outlook which mistrusted Hertzog's stance of 'South Africa first' with its connotations of republicanism. These men, led by Colonel Stallard, formed the even smaller Dominion Party, which was really a reversion to the standpoint of the old Unionists.

Mrs. Ballinger, the distinguished member of that hardy band of former Native Representatives, has pointed out that the small size of the Opposition was not altogether a disadvantage for it in facing the much larger Government coalition.[9] The Purified Nationalists had a discipline, cohesiveness, and single-mindedness that rendered them a formidable political foe. They at once began to exploit the colour

question, presenting themselves as the populist champions of the poor-
Whites against a government which, dominated by the 'imperialist'
gold-mines, had gone 'soft' on the Blacks. Here one easily recognizes
the old line of the English-speaking Labour Party. But then, in
addition, the Purifieds addressed themselves to Afrikaner youth, to a
rising generation which had not fought in the South African War. As
is commonly the case, they relived its iniquities more intensely than
the men who had actually fought in it. A movement to revive Afrikaner
nationalism broke forth around 1936, of which the Purified Nationalists
sought to become the political arm and expression.[10] This movement
readily appealed, like the Parti Québecois in Canada, to the passions
which could be mobilized about all those grievances, real and
imaginary, grounded in Afrikaner inequality and even the fear for
Afrikaner survival itself. Very rapidly the Purified Nationalists began
to capture the adherence not only of the Dutch Reformed clergy
but also of the Afrikaans teaching profession and the Afrikaans
press. In the first election which took place after the formation of
the United Party (1938) the Purifieds increased their strength to 27
seats.

All this notwithstanding, the question which I posed at the beginning
of the chapter is whether, looked at *before the fact*, this rise of Afrikaner
militancy signified its inevitable political victory. Or, to raise another
intertwined question, could the United Party, had the two elements of
the original coalition held together, have moved to resolve the race
problem without handing an electoral victory to the Purified Nationalists? Since we would have to be able to undo history in order to
'answer' this question with finality, what we are really asking is, first,
what did the main elements in the coalition really think about racial
policy and, second, what destroyed the coalition?

The major action of the United Party coalition was the enactment in
1936 of the policy known as 'segregation'. While I shall go into further
detail about the rise of this policy in the next chapter, I must say only
enough about it now to make the ensuing argument intelligible. The
crucial question is whether the men of 1936 were consciously legislating
a policy that was, as the Nationalists later contended, the forerunner of
apartheid. If the answer is yes, then the Nationalists can properly be
seen as the advance guard of White public opinion in South Africa;
and the thesis of their inevitable victory, *on their policy of apartheid*,
seems irrefutable. A whole generation of historians in South Africa
has seen the segregation policy precisely in this light, namely, as an
anticipation of what later became projected as Bantustans. And, indeed,

when we look at the main features of the former we can readily understand why.

The segregation policy had two main elements, a negative and a
positive. The former drew upon the fear of the Whites of being outvoted by the numerically superior Black population. This fear was
assuaged by legislation terminating any possible extension of the long-
standing non-racial franchise in the Cape (for Blacks) to the rest of the
Union. The Blacks in the Cape, which was the only province in which
they enjoyed the franchise, were taken off the common electoral roll
and transferred to a separate roll to elect three White representatives
to the House of Assembly. In the rest of the Union, where blacks were
previously altogether unrepresented, they were given four Representatives in the Senate. In addition to this the Union-wide Natives
Representative Council was established, partly elective and partly
appointed, which was to be regularly consulted about all legislation
concerning Blacks. The positive element of the segregation policy was
conceived curiously as a *quid pro quo* for removing the Blacks in the Cape
itself from the common roll, which, as the debates on the legislation
concerned showed, was not lightly entertained. This positive was the
addition of more land to the Native reserves, which were indicated as
the locus of Black economic and political development. Here one sees
the 'obvious' origin of the Bantustan idea.

As obvious as this judgement may seem, however, it abstracts from
the temporal context. Hence it overlooks one very important fact. This
is the assumptions in the minds of the men of 1936 about what kind of
a country South Africa, in economic respects, was. The predominant
opinion *of the time* was that South Africa was and would continue to
remain primarily agricultural and relatively poor at that. This was a
view that had evidently not fully recognized the force of the industrial
revolution that was taking place in South Africa. The Blacks in the
towns, who were seen as taking away jobs from poor-Whites, should
be sent back to the reserves. There they could be generously accom-
modated by the addition of more land. As for the poor-Whites themselves, they too, after the momentary relief of employment on the
'perishing assets' of the mines, would also eventually return to the
land.[11] That this view of what was actually taking place in South Africa
was anachronistic at the time of the 1936 legislation will be made fully
clear in the next chapter. What is alone under consideration at this
point is the question whether, as the new economic reality of a
permanent dependence of the urban industrial economy upon Black
labour impinged upon public opinion—and it was to do so very shortly

—a successful adaptation of policy to take account of this new reality could be made within the United Party structure. On this score we merely have to cite two key facts.

The first is that for the few years after 1936 during which Hertzog was still Prime Minister, the Natives Representative Council was working rather well. Black leadership in South Africa had profoundly and articulately opposed the 1936 legislation abridging their political rights in the Cape. In fact it was because of their protests, including a personal deputation to Hertzog himself, that the latter switched his mind in the last stages of the debate and agreed to preserve the existing Black franchise in the Cape, if on a separate electoral roll, rather than eliminating it altogether. The Black leaders grudgingly accepted this as better than nothing. But still, as Mrs. Ballinger pointed out, they were prepared to give the new framework a chance. And so long as they had confidence in the good faith of the government, effective consultation could and did take place. As she also pointed out, the Black members of the Natives Representative Council were impressed by the complexity of the details with which they had to deal once they got, so to speak, 'inside' the government.[12] Sooner or later, of course, consultation would have had to focus upon the delusions and also iniquities of the segregation policy, the hardships of which fell entirely upon the shoulders of the Blacks. Was moderate change in this respect so inconceivable?

Here I cite the second of the two facts. This is that the clearest statement about the outmoded character of the economic assumptions at the root of the segregation policy was made in 1948 by the late Chief Justice Fagan (1889–1963). Though appointed as Chairman of the Native Laws Commission by the Smuts Government, Fagan had in fact come not from that wing but from the Hertzog wing of the United Party. Regardless of what Hertzog (and that moderate part of Afrikaner nationalism he represented) may have thought in 1924 or in 1936, there is no reason to assume that Fagan, who had his roots in this selfsame wing of public opinion, could not have made clear to it what the real facts and issues were, *provided this wing of opinion was still part of the Government coalition*. There is no reason to assume that South Africa was then as bereft of common sense as it later appeared to become under the post–1948 Nationalist regime. One may readily concede that if the coalition had held together and had proceeded to modify the segregation policy to take account in some moderate way of the permanence of the urban Black labour force, it would have run into heavy weather from the Purified Nationalists. Exploiting the colour issue, they would have continued to attack the Government, as they did, for endangering the White man. And if this is linked together with those other issues connected with Afrikaner ethnic sentiment, such as socio-economic inequality *vis-à-vis* the English, they would probably have augmented their strength to 40, 50, or even 60 seats. In the meantime, however, South Africa would have begun to move towards a settlement of its race problem, which (as one can see from comparable experience elsewhere) would have moderated the extremist character of this political force.

I have sketched this 'model' of historical reconstruction, not obviously to try to 'undo' history, but to make clear what really happened in South Africa and why it is still pertinent to the present situation. This was that Afrikaner nationalism broke loose to become something like a wild and politically irresponsible force. The cause was not primarily the race problem, however much this wild force became obsessed on that account with its irrational and impracticable policy. It was rather the fact that the moderate wing of Afrikaner nationalism was discredited and politically undermined by the outbreak of the Second World War, which was seen much the same way in South Africa as it was in Quebec. Given the fact, however, that the Afrikaners were 60% of the White population, the political significance of the cleavage created by the decisions about the war had a national magnitude in South Africa it did not have in Canada. The essential point is that the Hertzog Nationalists and *a fortiori* the Malan Nationalists regarded the war, at the time of its immediate outbreak, as a British or European affair. Hence, for both wings, the neutrality of South Africa was at the very least a 'test' of its independence from British Empire concerns. And for the Malanites it was much more.

When Hertzog presented a resolution of neutrality to the House, he lost by a vote of 67 to 80. Voting with Hertzog's wing of the United Party were the Purified Nationalists led by Dr. Malan. The declaration of war, into which they saw South Africa dragged against the interest and the will of the *ware* Afrikaners, was, of course, grist for their mill. Voting with Smuts's wing of the United Party, which had increased its strength within the fusion in the 1938 election, were the English-speaking Dominion and Labour Parties.[13] Hertzog then advised the Governor-General to dissolve the House and call a new election. Ruling however, that the House had spoken and that Smuts could form a government in this crisis, the Governor-General appointed Smuts as Prime Minister, and he held this office throughout the war.

Toppled from power, Hertzog and his supporters then took their place on the Opposition benches along with the Purified Nationalists. But the former were still in a kind of limbo. While they had broken with Smuts on the war issue, they could not really fuse with the Purified Nationalists either, who never ceased to regard Hertzog as a man who had betrayed the Afrikaans cause. Hertzog, on his part, as much as Smuts, despised the Broederbond, the secret organization interlocked with the Purified National Party, for its narrow ethnic partisanship. None the less, they all put on a front and agreed in 1940 to re-unify the National Party, which styled itself thereafter the Herenigde [Re-united] Nasionale Party. Not long after this, however, Hertzog was repudiated by his own Free State Congress, which had been captured by the Malanites, when he opposed a policy stand compromising the rights of English-speaking South Africans. The bottom rail had got on top. He then withdrew from politics and died not long after, an embittered man.

Dr. Malan now saw the opportunity to realize his aim of making the H.N.P. the sole political arm of Afrikaner nationalism. But his position was by no means solid. Beyond the H.N.P. (which I shall hereafter call the National Party) and outside the parliamentary structure stood the Ossewa Brandwag (Ox-Wagon Sentinel), a para-military organization, and a few anti-constitutional parties, such as the New Order, whose leaders included a number of outright admirers of the Nazis. All these were rivals in the scramble for power precipitated by the collapse of Hertzog.[14] This entire wing of Afrikaner nationalism fully expected, until about 1944, that there would be a German victory in Europe, and with this the opportunity to re-establish an Afrikaner republic in South Africa. Malan and his Transvaal lieutenant Strijdom, however, prudently saw the crucial line to be drawn between constitutional and unconstitutional change. In this one decisive respect they followed in the footsteps not of the generals who raised the rebellion during the First World War but of Hertzog himself. In the election of 1943 Malan defeated candidates put up by all these organizations, increasing his strength to 43 seats. A journalist who accompanied him on this campaign told me that in every speech Malan made he deftly managed to turn his remarks into an attack upon the Ossewa Brandwag (O.B.), which had been by no means an unpopular organization. Then there was the Afrikaner Party. This had been formed by Hertzog's lieutenant N. C. Havenga out of the remnant of Hertzog's personal following, after Hertzog's rejection by the Malan Nationalists. This party also ran candidates in the 1943 election, who were all defeated, including Havenga himself. It did, however, have enough strength to let in the United Party in a few of the seats it contested.[15]

In this same election Smuts was returned to power. Whatever Smuts thought about the significance of this victory for himself and the future of the United Party, the election results showed that Malan, having put down all his Afrikaner nationalist rivals, was beginning to pull into his party the vote that had formerly gone to Hertzog. This could be seen not only in the weak performance of the Afrikaner Party. It was also seen in a by-election in Wakkerstroom the following year, in which the Nationalists recaptured from the United Party a seat that had been one of Hertzog's prior to the fusion.[16] The fact was that Smuts's United Party, after the departure of the Hertzog wing, was no longer the same. It had returned in a way to being the old coalition of *Bloedsappe* (literally, blood South African Party men)—that is, Afrikaners who had a hereditary loyalty to Botha and Smuts—and English which came together after Hertzog had split from the South African Party. While this coalition proved able to govern South Africa during both World Wars, it had a similar political liability at the end of each. This was the absence of a clear-cut link with any representative of moderate Afrikaner nationalism.

At this point Smuts made the first of two failures of omission which Mrs. Ballinger regarded as 'worse than a major tragedy'. By 1944, with the United States in the war and Holland long since overrun, and when, with many Afrikaners in the South African army, the character of the war was clear to all except the most fanatical extreme of Afrikaner nationalism, Smuts could have restored the bridge to the Hertzog wing of Afrikaner nationalism by bringing Havenga back into the United Party. Havenga was waiting for the invitation.

Mrs. Ballinger recorded a conversation which she had with Havenga in Johannesburg in 1944. She asked him when he was going to come back to 'us', meaning, as she indicated, the party he had left and Parliament:

His retort was immediate and, I felt, tinged with some not unnatural bitterness. 'Oh, they don't want me,' he said, referring to his former colleagues. I said I thought that was a very great pity, and had perforce to leave the matter there.[17]

She went on to say that some years later she had an occasion to tell this story to Mrs. Bertha Solomon, who represented the Johannesburg constituency of Jeppe:

[Mrs. Solomon] then told me that she had had much the same conversation with Mr. Havenga. . . . In due course she repeated the conversation to Mr. Hofmeyr and asked him why the leaders of the [United] Party did not get

Mr. Havenga back with them. To this Mr. Hofmeyr's reply was, 'Why should we? What has he to give?'

If this was indeed the attitude of the old United Party leaders, it reflected signally bad judgement on their part.[18]

Mrs. Ballinger saw that Havenga was the key figure in any possible reconstitution of the United Party coalition. As was shown in the election of 1943, he was too weak politically to stand by himself. She correctly foresaw, furthermore, that if Smuts did not bring him back into the United Party the only way he would be able to re-enter political life would be via the National Party. But whereas, in a coalition whose impulse came from Smuts, Havenga could play a moderating role, within the National Party he would be overpowered by the extremists.

All this was exactly what took place in and after 1948. To begin with, the Nationalists had not even expected to win this election in which, campaigning on the twin menaces of Communism and 'the rising tide of colour', they first projected their racial policy of apartheid.[19] In the background to this election lay a deteriorating racial situation. We need not repeat those details which Professor Kenneth Heard has so lucidly described. It suffices to point out that by the end of the war the segregation policy was a visible failure. It had not halted the pull of Black workers into the urban areas, where they had no security of status; and the land that had been promised them under the segregation policy as a *quid pro quo* had not been given them. Since neither Smuts nor his deputy, Hofmeyr, after the departure of the Hertzogites from the United Party, had the power-base with which to make the necessary changes in policy, relations between the Government and the Natives Representative Council broke down completely. The Council, after concluding that it was talking into a 'toy telephone', adjourned in August 1946. It then met with Hofmeyr in November, and with Smuts himself in May of the following year. Smuts spoke about expanding the authority of the Council and linking it up with the advisory boards in the urban townships to make it a 'Native Government which will be unified for the whole country'.[20] The Blacks saw that this was irrelevant to their concrete grievances. Councillor Thema, for example stated:

The majority of my people don't want to come to Parliament—I want that, but not the majority of my people—but they want something done which *they* can feel. If the Pass Laws, for instance, had been abolished, they would have been satisfied. It is things like that which make our people unhappy. My people won't feel as though they have gained anything very much if the Natives Representative Council is improved, but if the restriction of their movements is removed, they will be happy—and unless and until that is done they will never understand.[21]

Smuts had appointed the Fagan Commission, to which the question of the Pass Laws, among other things, had been referred, which was conducting its hearings at the time of this very meeting. We may surmise that he was waiting for it to report, which it did shortly before the 1948 election. We may also surmise that Smuts was expecting to get a real mandate before proceeding to implement its recommendations, which would have met those grievances of the Blacks which required a change of policy. I come to this in a moment.

Expressions of Black protest, not to mention the complications of the Indian problem in Natal for the United Party, were readily exploited as campaign issues by the Nationalists.[22] Yet in 1948 they polled only a minority of the popular vote, and were aided in their parliamentary representation by favourable delimitations that Smuts had been advised to change. They did not even win a parliamentary majority. They were able to form a government only in coalition with the nine newly elected members of Havenga's Afrikaner Party, which had made an alliance with the Nationalists for this election. This was an uneasy coalition, bearing in mind the repudiation of Hertzog by the Malan Nationalists in the Free State Congress of 1940. Within a short time the not unexpected happened. Havenga let it be known that he would like to get out of the Nationalist 'kraal'. His intermediary was Dr. E. G. Malherbe, who at once wrote a lengthy letter to Smuts that began with a reflection about the gravity of the crisis posed for South Africa and for 'our people' (that is, *ons volk*) by the victory of this extremist Government.[23] Malherbe, as a friend and distant kinsman, took the liberty of pointing out to Smuts the bold political step he would have to take if he were to save South Africa from being 'ruined'. In his letter he made clear that there was no longer any question of bringing Havenga 'into' the United Party. This was because '*the United Party as such is finished*'. Notwithstanding its war record, the United Party had become an 'old piece of machinery' that could never again govern the country in peace. It had 'no positive, aggressive policy'. It did not 'protect and foster the moderate elements in its own circles', whose support it took 'too much for granted'. This was shown by the way it permitted the bilingual-school policy to be torpedoed by the English jingoes on the one hand and the Broederbond on the other. It had shown 'no sign of rejuvenation'. It had lost its hold on the young people and so had 'no future'. But, as Malherbe further pointed out, the Nationalists were also in difficulties. The Broeders, the non-Broeder Nationalists, and the O.B.s were very divided among themselves in an atmosphere of suspicion and mutual distrust. At that moment the majority of the South African people were yearning for a leadership which could bind the country together. What was needed was nothing less than for Smuts and Havenga to abandon party identities, draw up a programme of principles, the core of which would be '*the building up and expansion of Western civilization in Southern Africa*', and then go together to the country. Malherbe spelled out the following key points in this programme:

(a) co-operation between the English- and Afrikaans-speaking sections;
(b) the economic development of South Africa in agriculture and industry;
(c) a progressive immigration policy, not only to build up the numbers of the White race, but also because we desperately need trained people to realize (b);
(d) the uplifting—economically and educationally—of the non-White population without which (b) is impossible; (Indeed, history has shown that the only guarantee for the survival of any civilization is its expansion and propagation among those who live together in its territory and among majority groups on its borders. This will necessarily be a gradual process.)
(e) the maintenance of our democratic way of life and the combating of Fascism, whether in the form of a Broederbond–Gestapo government, or in the form of totalitarian Communism.[24]

The big obstacle in the way of this political breakthrough was Smuts's perception of Havenga and his followers as 'a lot of Fascists'. In the flux within Afrikaner nationalism that still existed, an alliance of sorts had indeed arisen between Havenga and the remnants of the O.B. Malherbe did not mince words in telling Smuts that his evaluation of the situation was 'superficial', which he ascribed to the weakness of his information service:

The facts are as follows:
(1) Havenga uses the O.B. chiefly to intimidate the Nats. and to strengthen his bargaining power, and not because he has liking for the O.B.s or their ideology. Besides, with the exception of a small group of ideological leaders, Fascism does not penetrate very deeply into the rank and file of the O.B.s. It is not in the nature of our people and does not fit in with our indigenous institutions. . . . I would, therefore, not attach too much weight to Havenga's opportunistic affiliation with the 'Fascists'.
(2) Havenga hates the *Broederbond*. It was they who stabbed his old friend, General Hertzog, in the back. That he will never forgive them.[25]

But then there was the question of what to do with Hofmeyr, the liberal member of Smuts's Cabinet, who, as the quotations from Mrs. Ballinger's book suggest, was the probable source of Smuts's 'information service'. Malherbe told Smuts frankly that Hofmeyr would be an 'indigestible lump' in the make-up of the centre:

This brings me to the great problem of what to do with Mr. Hofmeyr. I have the highest regard for his high ideals and administrative ability. He was by far the ablest member of your cabinet. But, as a result of his emphasis at this particular time on abstract ideals regarding the non-Whites (ideals which history will one day, when we are all dead, prove to be absolutely right), the Nationalists made a caricature of him and his ideas and built up such a mental stereotype in the public mind against him and his ideas that it will take years to get past it. Moreover, he is designated as your successor and prime minister. This was probably the chief factor that contributed to the defeat of the United Party in the rural areas. At any rate the Nationalists ascribe their unexpected victory mainly to this. (This point is probably already a common-place to you!) The fact remains, however, that Hofmeyr will be an embarrass-ment in any attempt to forge into one solid, central group the greater number of United Party supporters and the moderate elements that Mr. Havenga will bring with him. However much we may deplore it, we cannot get past the fact that Hofmeyr will remain sticking, like an indigestible lump, in the stomach of such a group. It will inevitably cause serious crises sooner or later and shatter the whole thing. You will therefore be obliged, for the sake of the eventual realization of the ideals for which Hofmeyr strives, to leave him out, unless he gives in about those principles of his. I strongly doubt whether he will do so. He will probably take a few liberal elements with him but one could always rely upon them to support the central party if it were to come to a serious contest with the extremist elements who now dominate the present government and who, in my opinion, would have hardly one-third of the country's voters behind them if a new central party under you and Havenga can be formed. In the course of time the Hofmeyr stereotype will fade and he can, in all likelihood, return. The realization of his ideals is a matter of the gradual education of the people and will, even under favourable leadership, take years. Under the policy of the present government the clock is not only being put back, but there could easily be revolution and bloodshed. That you, at this time of threatening danger, should not be ready to make great sacrifices as regards persons will be disastrous for our people and our democratic institutions—not to mention Mr. Hofmeyr's own liberal ideas. He should see this.[26]

But to drop Hofmeyr was not the greatest sacrifice that Smuts would have to make. Malherbe tactfully indicated that to make this new coalition a reality Smuts might well have to serve under Havenga in an act equal in its magnanimity to his decision in 1933. In the 'evening star of his career', this alone was what could save South Africa and 'our people' from a great disaster.[27]

This letter of Malherbe to Smuts is the single most important piece of documentary evidence against the thesis of the 'historical inevita-bility' of the post–1948 Nationalist regime. The only qualification that one might make of Malherbe's analysis of the facts is this: even if Smuts and Havenga—whose break with the Government would have brought it down—had gone to the country and yet failed to prevent the re-election of the Nationalists, they would have brought into being a virile and coherent Opposition, whose impact upon public opinion would have been something that the Nationalists would have always to take seriously. Its existence, therefore, would in itself have checked the extremism of the post-1948 regime.

Smuts's reply to Malherbe was a very brief letter in which, without even mentioning Havenga's name, he dismissed an alliance between the United Party and 'the O.B.' as 'rather odd'.[28] In part it was the *broedertwis* (brothers' quarrel) at work. The Afrikaner could never forgive the fellow Afrikaner for what Mrs. Ballinger and Mrs. Solomon did not even deign to notice. But then, as Dr. Malherbe told me, there was a personal element. Smuts had lost his seat in the election in Standerton, which embittered him. His son had died. And he was a very old man. Had he been twenty years younger, it would have been a different story.

1948–1960: The centre overpowered

The Nationalists were thus in power, and would stay there, aided by favourable delimitations which they would make even more so. The United Party did not hesitate to call attention to the part played by these delimitations, a charge which Nationalist supporters regarded as 'sour grapes'. In fact, the latter were right but for the wrong reasons. If the United Party had taken power in 1948 and remained the wartime coalition of *Bloedsappe* and diverse groups of English, it would have disintegrated in office rather than in opposition. It is with an eye to this alone that many people in South Africa have concluded that the Nationalist victory had been inevitable, if not in 1948, then in 1953. But such a conclusion disregards the decisive political fact in the situation along the lines indicated by Malherbe. This was not really the question which party won in 1948. It was rather that Smuts did not act at the only possible moment to depose *both* parties, or the existing bi-party *structure*, so as to bring into being a restored centre, in which moderate Afrikaner nationalism would once again find a political home. Only if this had been done would a South African government have been able to address itself to the race problem in a moderate and non-extreme way. South Africa was at this stage in something like the position of the United States South after the Civil War, when Lincoln was the one man in the country who had the authority and the prestige to moderate and curb the vindictiveness of the Southern Whites towards their former slaves and the vindictiveness of the Northern radicals towards the former 'rebels'.[29] With his chance death there was no one who could prevent the extremes from triggering a chain reaction, culminating in the punitive Reconstruction that set back race relations for fifty, or perhaps a hundred years.

In South Africa Smuts was in a parallel position. He had to take the lead if the constituent elements of the old United Party fusion were to be reunited. And he could do this only at that one moment when the opportunity was ripe. This was while the Nationalists were still dependent upon Havenga's tiny Afrikaner Party, a dependence from which they shortly freed themselves, after the integration of the 6 (all Nationalist) South West African constituencies. And the incredible thing is that this embittered hero, rejected even by his own constituency, did not realize it! His failure to respond to Havenga's overtures was, in the words of Talleyrand, worse than a crime. It was a mistake. For this had the most profound effect upon South African politics, from which the nation is still struggling to liberate itself. The party structure of government and opposition acquired abnormal characteristics: not those of a country which is polarized because a centre does not exist, but rather one which has *become* polarized, because the centre has been either overpowered or cannot be reached by the leading political alternatives. This polarization, which precipitated itself about race policy, took place via an ethnic polarization between Afrikaner and English.

Once the moderate Hertzogite Afrikaners, who would have rallied around a restored centre party, had been spurned, a power vacuum, or to be more precise a political anomaly, was created in South Africa. This anomaly lay in the fact that the Nationalists, because of the overweighting of the rural vote and the overconcentration (that is, anything more than 51%) of the United Party vote in their own constituencies, had a minority of the popular vote. The United Party, although declining in strength, continued to outpoll the National Party right until the 1961 election. This was a state of affairs that the Government understandably wanted to change. Yet, as the Nationalists looked at the United Party, they could take the measure of its efficacy by its treatment of Havenga, who by 1949 had lost any power to reshape a coalition. Furthermore, as the Nationalists looked at the English in South Africa, they saw that the latter, not unlike the Yankees in Boston, would be quite prepared to acquiesce in a regime in which

2

Table 2

Percentage of total votes polled for main parties, 1938–74

Party	1938	1943	1948	1953	1958	1961[a]	1966	1970	1974
National[b]	29·56	33·66	36·37	45·50	48·34	57·12	59·96	54·43	50·5
Afrikaner	—	—	3·59	—	—	—	—	—	—
United	54·42	53·18	50·38	51·62	51·03	33·95	36·22	37·23	35·0
Progressive	—	—	—	—	—	4·96	2·74	3·43	7·4
Labour	5·06	4·12	2·76	2·78	—	—	—	—	—
Independents	5·51	5·51	6·90	0·10	0·62	1·39	—	—	—
Dominion	6·08	—	—	—	—	1·08	—	—	—
National Union	—	—	—	—	—	2·58	—	—	—
H.N.P.	—	—	—	—	—	—	—	3·56	3·2
Democratic	—	—	—	—	—	—	—	—	1·4

Sources: *Star* 'Election Booklet' (1970) and *Star*, 25 April 1974.

Notes: (a) In 1961 there was an unusually high number of uncontested seats: National Party 50, and United Party 20.
(b) See Note (b) to Table 1.

they did not have a real voice, provided that their interests and rights were not threatened.[30] Because of the fact that Afrikaners were a majority of the Whites (though not of the Whites and Coloureds taken together), the Nationalists could proceed to fulfil what had been only a hope or a dream when they formed the Purified National Party. This was to weld together the Afrikaner vote into a majority of the electorate under the umbrella of Afrikaner nationalism. In this way they could regain by constitutional means what 'they lost on the battlefield'.

From today's standpoint with their evident success, people are inclined to say, 'How could the Nationalists have failed to mobilize such an irresistible force?' But, as I stated at the very outset of this book, this unabashedly sectionalist aim did not possess a guarantee of automatic success. It possessed this neither before nor even, which is more interesting, after the Nationalists took power. Malherbe correctly foresaw that the Nationalists would begin to project their extreme policies as the moderate course in order to attract the votes of the Afrikaner moderates (and even some English votes).[31] To do this they had to make the case—essentially, by projecting the centre as a dangerous extreme—that their own policy was sane and sober, and the only alternative. But this took time. For their policy not only encountered the resistance of the English press and of world opinion. It also had to wrestle with the 'South Africanist' sentiments and the common sense of Afrikaners, who, unlike these two, had the votes which the National Party was seeking.

In a number of respects the Nationalists, once in power, really did drop the extremist standpoints they had held in their days of opposition. In the first place the old isolationism of Afrikaner nationalism, which had looked upon world affairs through the prism of their putative bearing upon British imperialism, vanished virtually overnight. The Government was absolutely at one with Churchill, Truman, and Smuts on the Cold War. In fact, it sent a contingent of troops to Korea in consonance with the United Nations resolution. In education, it is true, the Government terminated dual-medium and parallel-medium education, where children of both language groups went to the same school. It replaced this with a system of compulsory mother-tongue instruction, the political intention of which was to compel Afrikaans-speaking children, including those who came from families which were effectively bilingual, to attend separate Afrikaans schools. Since the Afrikaans teaching profession was virtually all Nationalist, and since the Afrikaners stood to the English in a 60–40 ratio, the political implications of this, which would be realized in about twelve years, were obvious. But, as Malherbe's letter to Smuts pointed out, the English 'jingoes' had never given the support to bilingualism in education needed to counter this attack upon it from the other side. The Broederbond, when the Nationalists were still in opposition, sent out a secret message advising its members not to press too strenuously for separate schools. 'The English', as the message stated, 'are winning the battle for us.'[32]

On another tack Jews had been excluded from membership in the Transvaal branch of the National Party. Within a few years after 1948, this exclusion—which never corresponded to the cordial relations between Jews and Afrikaners on the *platteland* in any event—was dropped; and there were even a few Jews elected as Nationalist mayors in Transvaal towns. Finally we must note that another of their old extremist positions, the populist sabre-rattling about nationalizing the gold mines, had disappeared from the Nationalist press.

But still, this was an all-Afrikaner government, for the first time in the history of Union politics. It immediately shelved Smuts's plans for large-scale government-assisted immigration from Europe (which went instead to Australia and Canada) for fear that the Afrikaner would be 'ploughed under'. The primary sphere, however, in which the extremism of the Nationalists has so manifestly overpowered the South African political centre has been in that of race policy. But, without further ado, what was this centre? Like all centres in constitutional governments it is that position which 'removes a vast mass of evil without shocking a vast mass of prejudice'. It thus dilutes abstract principle in taking cognizance of the most potent prejudices or opinions of the moment so as to *move* that society as far as possible towards the political good demanded by that principle. Its guidance by that principle thus distinguishes a true centre from a compromise that is no more than acquiescence in an unjust *status quo*. But what principles has this centre been guided by on the race question? We must clarify this point in order to have a standard for judging, not only what the Nationalists said, but also what they did. With such a standard we can see where they conformed to as well as where they deviated from the requirements of this centre, whether they wanted to or not. Only by holding fast to this standard can we look below the cloak of overpowering rhetoric and counter-rhetoric which has become such an integral part of South African politics.

The clearest exposition of this centre remains, notwithstanding the volumes of words uttered and printed about race relations in South Africa, the Fagan Report, or the *Report of the Native Laws Commission*

(1946-8). This was the Commission which Smuts appointed in the last years of his administration to inquire into the status of the Blacks in the towns, which was and still is the unresolved problem at the heart of the apartheid policy.

This Report (supplemented by Fagan's political writings) was the quintessence of practical common sense. As Fagan reviewed the racial situation that had evolved during this century, he saw that the urban South African economy had become dependent upon Black labour and that an important segment of the latter was now a permanently settled part of the labour force. At the beginning of the industrial revolution, at the time of the first diamond diggings, this was not the case. In this early phase the Black labour employed was still fully attached to tribal life, and sought work only on an intermittent or migratory basis. In radical contrast to the atmosphere in South Africa today, when government policy is obsessed by the spectre of a mass influx into the towns of Black work-seekers, the problem for industry as late as the end of the South African War was how to lure and even compel Blacks to seek work and to stay there on a regular basis.[33] For no industrial employer ever really wanted migratory or casual labour, except for seasonal work. While industry was becoming more technologically advanced, however, the Blacks themselves were acquiring the tastes and habits of workers in settled urban communities. By the 1920s it was massively apparent that an urban Black labour force was in existence which required a policy to regulate it. Among other things there was the question of sanitation and hygiene. A plague had broken out in Johannesburg in the squatter-camps that had taken shape for Black habitation.

The legislation enacted to deal with these new conditions was the Natives (Urban Areas) Act of 1923. For the present I call attention only to a central point. This is that when the Transvaal Local Government (or Stallard) Commission of 1922, whose conclusions were the foundations of the policy embodied in the Act, came to define the legal status of the Blacks in the towns, it laid down the dictum that all Blacks in the towns were essentially migratory workers:

If the Native is to be regarded as a permanent element in municipal areas, and if he is to have an equal opportunity of establishing himself there permanently, there can be no justification for basing his exclusion from the franchise on the simple ground of colour.

Some Coloured persons and Natives are possessed of property and brains, and have educational qualifications not inferior to some enfranchised Europeans; many carry on trades and are their own employers, and it cannot be denied that they have special and peculiar needs not at present being met.

If, as we consider, it is to the public advantage that all sections of the permanent community should be represented in government, on what ground is the franchise withheld from the Natives?

We consider that the history of the races, especially having regard to South African history, shows that the commingling of Black and White is undesirable. The Native should only be allowed to enter urban areas, which are essentially the White man's creation, when he is willing to enter and to minister to the needs of the White man, and should depart therefrom when he ceases so to minister.[34]

Fagan saw that by the late 1940s this policy had become a fiction that could not fail to produce hardships for the permanently settled Black townsman. He also saw that the foundation of this policy was not malice but fear on the part of the Whites of being swamped by a common franchise, aggravated by the fear of the 'slippery slope'. The latter was the White's belief that if they but recognized the non-migratory Blacks in the towns as permanent, they would not only have to grant them the vote on a common franchise, but slide all the way down the slope to total fusion or 'commingling of the races'. They were unwilling to do this. Therefore, they would declare the Blacks to be strangers who were not entitled to the normal rights of settled labour such as freehold property. The complement to this was the doctrine that the Blacks could enjoy such rights only in their own 'segregated' reserves (or 'homelands'), to which they would eventually return.

Fagan contended that this argument 'puts the cart before the horse':

To deny a home to the Native because he may not have the vote along with the White man, and then to base his exclusion from the franchise on the fact that the town is not his home, is a most transparent camouflaging of the true reason for his exclusion. The real reason is still the racial difference, and the faulty reasoning we have analysed above merely leads to other privileges also being withheld from the Native in order to provide an apparent reason for his exclusion from the franchise. And if the difference in race is indeed the real reason for excluding him from the franchise, why not say so? Then the other questions can be dealt with on their merits: the question whether he may have a home in the urban area or as a fact already has one; the question, if he is a settled resident, what rights and privileges should accrue to him as such; and the question whether there cannot be alternative arrangements which will give him those rights without undesirable commingling between the races.[35]

As Fagan contended, the massive ethnic and social heterogeneity of the population was a circumstantial fact that had to be faced as clearly as the permanence of a large number of Blacks in the urban areas. And it was the inability of the Stallard Commission to deal with the first that made it unable to deal with the second:

The Stallard Commission sat at a time when *the principle of separate institutions for the different races, where a division is practicable and where common institutions may lead to friction or to less efficient administration, linked with machinery for the expression and communication of views and for consultation with one another, was still relatively unknown*. . . . In actual practice that principle had always found a measure of recognition. Conditions in South Africa automatically brought that about. In people's minds, however, it was still so slightly or so vaguely formulated that they always tried to defend their application of it on other grounds, just as the Stallard Commission did, in order to try to reconcile it with *a conception of democracy which works well in countries with a more homogeneous population, but the adaptation of which to a country with so heterogeneous a population as we have in South Africa must inevitably involve some modification*.[36]

The essence of Fagan's practical or political perspective was, in sum, constituted by two insights which laid down the poles of the situation. The first was that the permanence of a settled Black labour force could neither be reversed nor denied. Hence, total segregation, in the sense of a partition with transfer of populations, was impossible. Thus a policy which projected this aim as a basis for denying the Black townsmen the civic rights of settled labour could only create hardship and injustice, however 'sincere' the belief in the scheme. The second pole of Fagan's politics was his recognition of the political impossibility of instituting in South Africa the normal democratic franchise of one-man, one-vote, or as he termed it, majority rule by the counting of heads. His reasoning on this score was asserted only in political, not theoretical statements. This is that the common franchise, as it would work in South Africa, would not unite the citizenry but trigger an ethnic struggle for power with the consequent political destruction of the numerically smaller Whites. In fervid rhetoric he stated:

In South Africa we, the White men, cannot leave and cannot accept the role of a subject race.

To the Afrikaners, among whom I count myself, it would mean the destruction or the humiliation of a nation, of a language, of a national culture which has become part of our soul and our being.[37]

In other statements he pointed out less fervidly that even if *he* did not think that this would be the necessary outcome, the predominant part of White opinion did:

I refer to the question of franchise rights and of representation in the Central Parliament of the Bantu, and of change in the franchise and the representation of the Coloured people.

I am not going to spend any time in arguing the merits or demerits of this question. . . .[38]

For the purpose of this address my starting point is a simple acceptance of the fact that the majority of the White electorate—of the people who alone can constitutionally make the change—have shown themselves to be unequivocally opposed to any concession at all in this direction, and that I can see no sign of a softening of their mood in this regard. Anything savouring of an allocation of political power between Whites and non-Whites on the basis of a counting of heads is seen by them as opening a flood-gate which they wish to keep firmly bolted, and even an incipient gesture in that direction raises fears which will not yield to argument.[39]

If then total separation was impossible and normal political integration was equally impossible, what then was possible as a movement towards justice? And for Fagan this meant government by and with the consent, not virtual but actual, of the governed. We may recall the norm he laid down in his critique of the Stallard Commission: 'separate institutions for the different races . . . linked with machinery for the expression and communication of views and for consultation'. At first sight this may appear to be part and parcel of what the Nationalists called 'apartheid', which literally does in fact mean 'separateness'. But there are two things one must take into account to understand Fagan's policy. The first is the general consideration that such terms as 'separation', 'integration', and 'majority rule' can easily become formulas that are politically meaningless when abstracted from the context which indicates the political intentions of those who use them and the implications they have for political power. In Ulster, for example, even the Protestant extremists stand fast on the principle of majority rule. But the Protestants are a majority in Ulster. The appeal to majority rule in this case is, among other things, a basis of opposition to unification with the rest of Ireland and of resistance to being swamped by a Catholic majority. That the mere assertion of the principle, in legalistic ways, does not dispose of the problems within Ulster itself is as obvious as is the fact that in ethnically polarized societies majority rule can become or appear tyrannical, however much it conforms to a text-book notion of democracy as 'one-man, one-vote'. Justice, in other words, would require that the Catholic minority in Ulster feels that it has a voice in the regime. I will not comment on any of the proposals that have been advanced to bring this about. In the present context we are concerned only with pointing out that the principle in this case also has the above-mentioned external implication, or trans-legalistic, political content; and as experience has shown, this cannot be ignored.

On another tack we note that integration, in the United States during the first half of this century, meant 'open doors', freedom from discriminating laws which excluded or assigned individuals solely on the basis of race. Integration thus meant equality of opportunity, the career open to talent, or in a word, merit. So long as both state and social action was directed to this unambiguous and morally defensible goal, there was, notwithstanding long effort and struggle, steady progress and no reaction. Then, after legal segregation began to fall away, it became obvious that the disappearance of this framework did not bring about an instantaneous disappearance of those inequalities in inter-group averages that were easily attributable to discriminating inequality in the past. Nor did the relief from legal segregation see the disappearance of those ethnic sentiments and prejudices which manifest themselves in selective association in the private sphere, where, in a liberal democracy, they have an unassailable constitutional right. This is true despite the fact that private or social inequality can hardly avoid having some kind of spill-over into the public sphere, however much we try to draw a legitimate and clear-cut boundary between the two. Under the impress of a much more radical understanding of equality, however, the inequality in both the public and the private spheres began to be attacked with demands for instant solutions. Integration acquired a changed meaning, emphasis, or aim, without a clear-cut public awareness of the character of the change. From equality of opportunity for the equally qualified, it began to mean 'equality now', with the morally dubious (and politically impossible) premise that any disproportion in numbers on a group basis, first racial, then sexual, in any sphere, was proof of immoral 'segregation' or of discrimination in the here and now against individuals. Related to this, integration also became linked to the premise that racial heterogeneity or co-presence was something that was good for its own sake, rather than something that would be the natural outcome of individuals' pursuing their own goals in an atmosphere freed from racial restrictions. Normally, this change would have been noticed and resisted as it is beginning to be now. But the term 'segregation' had been so discredited by the victorious elimination of the segregation statutes that simply to call something 'segregated' was virtually to silence rational public discussion about these matters. This paralysed and confused not only the lower federal judiciary and the federal bureaucracy but the Black leadership itself. The effect of all this, however, was to turn the whole movement for racial (and also sexual) equality on its head.

To begin with, judges and bureaucrats, on the basis of the new meanings of integration, began to prescribe quotas on a racial basis even in employment. Whereas formerly an institution, let us say a university, was called integrated if it were known to be open to all on the basis of

merit, now one had to see and to count how many people of this group
or that group were actually 'represented' among the students and
faculty before one could say it was truly 'integrated'. But this introduction of Jim Crow into the public spheres of the universities and the
labour market conflicts with the very norm of a colour-blind legal
framework to which the leaders of the civil rights movement were and
still are, in their hearts and souls, one hundred per cent dedicated. Then
too judges began to require compulsory inter-neighbourhood bussing of
schoolchildren to bring about 'integration', that is, an administered
co-presence of different racial groups in the schools, in proportions
determined by them. This has encountered the most acute resistance
not only from outright bigots but from people, both White and Black,
who buy a house because they like the neighbourhood *and its school*.
Finally we note that on the basis of this new meaning of integration,
there is no clear-cut standard for ever deciding that a given institution
is 'integrated'. Since not only the proportions constituting a 'balanced'
co-presence but even the group definitions themselves are arbitrarily
decided, they can always be subsequently challenged. Any group can
arise and claim it is 'under-represented'. This is thus a formula for
permanent litigation and permanent convulsion. It is no surprise that
the issue is far from settled and that national leadership in the United
States is beginning to point the way back to what is in fact the original
meaning of integration, namely, freedom from the tyranny of
'ethnicity'.* In politics, all in all, the question of what something means
or how it works in the concrete is thus almost 'everything'.

The second and crucial point in Fagan's policy was 'machinery for
the expression and communication of views and for consultation'.
Fagan's racial policy had the definite intention, not of taking away
rights, but of conferring them upon the Blacks in the urban areas, the
lack of which was the cause of their most urgent grievances. In so far
as the arrangements he proposed outflanked the White fear of being
swamped, they would make it possible for Blacks to get an effective
voice in the defence of their interests, that would be the practical
equivalent of the franchise in a homogeneous polity. But let us be as
concrete as possible. Otherwise we will get lost in a welter of formulas,
abstractions, and rhetoric, which has been the unbroken characteristic

---

* The U.S. Supreme Court, on 25 June 1976, ruled that the provisions of the
1964 Civil Rights Act were 'not limited to discrimination against members of any
particular race'. In overruling a lower court decision that the 1964 statute was not
applicable to Whites, the high court said that the same criteria must be applied
equally to all races. This ruling is a return to the original meaning of integration.

of South African politics since even before the Nationalists came into power.

The Whites, Fagan stated, were unwilling to subject themselves to the possibility of being outvoted by the numerically superior Blacks in racially mixed legislatures or councils at any level—municipal, provincial, or national. As he noted, it was politically impossible to argue with the fear behind this resistance. But Fagan also thought that it was the absolute democratic right of the Whites to be apprehensive about being ethnically overpowered, and to resist any change towards such an eventuality. Constitutional democracy in an ethnically plural situation should not require a people to commit ethnic suicide just because they are in a minority. And as we shall see later, this point of his was only the surface of a profound democratic critique of legalistic majoritarianism.

But if democracy means government by consent of the governed, the Blacks too must clearly have a voice in the regime. Between the White fear of being swamped by a general franchise and the Black right to have a voice, where is the opening to be found, an opening which, when grabbed hold of and actualized, would in fact begin to normalize the political situation? Fagan answered this question in a succinct statement of principles, which, he contended, could guide policy, not only in respect of the Blacks, but also, 'with adaptation to the difference in circumstances', in respect of the other non-White groups as well. These 'rules' were as follows:

(1) In matters which do not affect other interests than their own, or which affect such other interests only to a relatively insignificant degree: the highest measure of self-administration of which they show themselves to be capable and which is compatible with the general safety and welfare of the State; and

(2) In all other matters in which they (as well as other racial groups) have an interest, consultation, and again consultation.[40]

Fagan went into all the essential detail about the precise *practical* meaning of these two rules.

The first rule would, as he put it, 'automatically' involve the grant of a much greater measure of self-government to the Blacks in the reserves than in the urban areas.[41] He also saw the prudence of this government being fashioned according to their own custom or choice, where traditional tribal institutions would be blended with modern parliamentary ones. The reason behind this was the basic geo-political fact that in the reserves—and not in all parts of them either—there were large homogeneous groups which had little contact in their day-to-day lives with other groups. Fagan went on to say that he regarded

local government in the reserves in no sense as a 'concession' based on
sentimental or ideological considerations, but simply as a reasoned
dictate of good administration. In fact, as he made clear in another
context, his whole policy was concerned not at all with 'making
concessions' but with doing the right thing.[42] Crucial to his standpoint
was his rejection as folly of a policy which saw the augmentation of
self-government in the reserves as some kind of a *quid pro quo* for
taking away rights from Blacks in the urban areas:

The policy of playing off the granting of such rights in the reserves against
the withholding of rights from the Bantu in other areas is one that I can
neither comprehend nor approve of. It is unrealistic, and there is a ring of
insincerity in it—as if we are looking for debating points and not for sound
administration. It also leads to wrong results *on both sides*. It is like giving
one man two coats, not because he needs them, but as an excuse for depriving
his brother of his only coat. The one will then be getting too much and the
other too little.

   We should indeed ask ourselves whether the open preaching of the playing-
off idea as part of our present policy is not in fact already leading us into the
danger I have indicated: that of making promises to the reserve chiefs, or
raising expectations in their minds, which are not based solely on their needs
and merits, but are motivated by the desire of being able to say: 'See what we
are giving the Bantu in their own areas; now those who are in our areas
should not complain of anything we deprive them of or of anything we do to
them.'[43]

This describes exactly the outlook of the Government after Dr.
Verwoerd acquired the direction of Bantu [Black] Administration.
The reader should keep these passages in mind in considering contemporary developments. For those chiefs in the reserves, who ultimately accepted the framework of the homelands as the only basis
of getting a voice in South African society, but who resisted a prema-
ture plunge into the 'independence' held out to them by the Government, proved to be more prudent and moderate than might have been
reasonably expected.

   The second rule concerned what Fagan termed the 'two top
priorities' that 'cannot wait'. These were the position of the urban
Blacks and a revision of the apartheid legislation affecting the
Coloureds and the Indians. These pithy sentences of his about these
'top priorities' date from 1963:

They have to be tackled *at once*.
They can be tackled without the Bantustans.
They can be tackled without franchise changes.
But—
they cannot be properly tackled without consultation with the people concerned.[44]

Now in the framework of Bantu administration which the Nationalists inherited, there was a rudimentary institution of local government
for Blacks in the urban townships, called 'advisory boards'. Like the
Natives Representative Council itself they had the weakness of all
advisory bodies without administrative powers or responsibilities.
They tended, when ignored, to become consumed by agitation against
the policy which relegated them to this status. Fagan, somewhat like
Smuts, saw that this could be partly corrected by the transformation
of these boards into organs of genuine local government. But there
could be no question here of 'fobbing the Blacks off' with local government, for the most elementary reason. This was that municipal administration, for Whites as for Blacks, could not be independent of higher
control.[45] While Fagan saw that effective administration required
consultation and liaison between Blacks and Whites on the local level,
this consultation would have to be carried on at every level of government, from top to bottom. Life in the municipalities could not be
disconnected from the overall policy of the country.

For Fagan consultation meant *effective* consultation. Resolutions
and petitions, presented to officials who had no authority to depart
from a pre-fixed policy, full of manifest iniquities—this was not
consultation but noise, or, in the words of Councillor Mosaka, 'talking
into a toy telephone'.[46] Nor, conversely, was it to be confused with
that pseudo-consultation where government officials would invite
Blacks to collaborate with them on a policy about which they had not
been consulted, and which injured their legitimate interests. Since the
breakdown of the Natives Representative Council, consultation had
come to acquire this meaning for many people in South Africa. But
could there be genuine consultation without equal power? And could
there be equality of power without the general franchise, which ran
once again into the familiar blank wall of South African politics? It is
here that Fagan's subtle mind saw a practical way of escaping from
what seemed to be a vicious circle. In Chapter IV, I shall discuss in a
theoretical light Fagan's grasp of the fact that a free parliament
depends for its proper functioning upon a free press. For the moment
it suffices to point out that, for Fagan, effective consultation between
Black and White on the highest level had to take place within bi-
partisan parliamentary committees, meeting regularly with Blacks,
under conditions which were the same as those surrounding parliamentary debate itself. That is, they would be open to the public and
covered by the press. In this way the Blacks could make their views
known, in such a manner as to affect public opinion. Thus they would

not merely feel but know that they were contributing to the formation
of overall policy. In the light of the events which have since taken
place, the following passage of Fagan's is of especial interest:

Whether we like ex-Chief Luthuli's views or not, we must admit that a very
substantial number of Bantu look up to him as their leader. Being a person
who has been prohibited from attending public gatherings, he falls under
section 19 of the General Law Amendment Act, 1962, which has just been
placed on the statute book.

This means that no one may record or publish any statement of his. He has
been rendered as silent as if he were dead; more so, for even past statements
of his are covered by the prohibition.

For my present purpose I shall assume, without admitting, that Luthuli's
utterances and messages might incite his followers to violent action and
should therefore be suppressed. But you should not plug a hole in a boiler
without inserting a safety valve. We shall be closing the mouths of many
Bantu by closing that of their spokesman.

Can we risk doing that—for our own sake as well as theirs? For we shall
not be stopping their thoughts; we shall only be cutting off our knowledge of
what they think.

Machinery such as I am proposing can provide opportunities for a man in
Luthuli's position to speak under conditions of security and control, where
every reasonable statement he makes can be considered and every unreasonable one be immediately answered and refuted.

The question of the time when, if ever, the reserves will reach the stage of
complete independence which the Prime Minister is holding out to them is
one which I shall not try to answer, and I do not think anyone else can
seriously do. What I am sure of, however, is that in all stages of limited or
full self-government through which they may pass, contacts which can help
them and us to correlate our policies and to co-operate with each other will
be both to their and to our advantage; and consultative machinery more or
less on the lines I have sketched would be the ideal means to that end.[47]

This may suffice for a sketch of Fagan's practical political proposals.

Against both the letter and the spirit of the Fagan Report, the
Nationalists made the cornerstone of their policy the doctrinaire
reassertion that there were only two alternatives—either total territorial
segregation or total integration on the basis of a general franchise.
While there was nothing novel about this formulation, which was in
fact a deduction from the Wilsonian idea of national self-determination,
it was first articulated as policy by the Nationalists in their pamphlet
Race Relations Policy of the National Party, issued in 1947, in anticipation of the 1948 election:

There are two distinct guiding principles determining the South African
policy affecting the non-Whites. One line of thought favours a policy of

integration, conferring equal rights—including the franchise as the non-Whites progressively become used to democratic institutions—on all civilised and educated citizens within the same political structure.

Opposed to this is the policy of apartheid, a concept historically derived from the experience of the established White population of the country, and in harmony with such Christian principles as justice and equity. It is a policy which sets itself the task of preserving and safeguarding the racial identity of the White population of the country; of likewise preserving and safeguarding the identity of the indigenous peoples as separate racial groups, with opportunities to develop into self-governing national units; of fostering the inculcation of national consciousness, self-esteem and mutual regard among the various races of the country.

The choice before us is one of these two divergent courses: either that of integration, which would in the long run amount to national suicide on the part of the Whites; or that of apartheid, which professes to preserve the identity and safeguard the future of every race, with complete scope for every one to develop its own sphere while maintaining its distinctive national character, in such a way that there will be no encroachment on the rights of others, and without a sense of being frustrated by the existence and development of others.[48]

Since the legal structure of apartheid which the Nationalists implemented has been thoroughly studied and is furthermore well known, we confine ourselves here to a few essential points.[49] The first is that the initial moves of the Nationalist Government after the 1948 election were entirely negative. From within its extremist, later termed *verkrampte* power-base, the new Government took steps to protect White labour and began an assault on anything that could be seen as social and political integration. In 1951, the Government moving forward with the policy it had advanced from its first years in opposition, began a protracted attempt to place the Coloured franchise in the Cape, which had supported the United Party under both Hertzog and Smuts, on a separate electoral roll. This took five years to accomplish. Since the Government lacked the statutory majority that was required to alter the Cape franchise by the South African Constitution, it resorted in the end to transparently unconstitutional procedures to do it. This tampering with the Constitution provoked the first open break with the National Party by some leading Nationalists. Side by side with this assault on the Coloured franchise the Government set about dismantling those features of the 1936 legislation which could be regarded as a 'halfway house', or concessions to integration.[50] Dr. Verwoerd, in his very first speech to the Senate, demanded the abolition of the Natives Representative Council, which admittedly had broken down under the Smuts Government. Disregarding the Fagan Report altogether, which he saw only through the prism of the 'two alternatives', he grabbed hold of Smuts's old idea of a 'unified Native Government' and then conjured up a spectre of 'two parliaments and two public services spread over a single country with agitation, clashes, and strife'.[51] But this notion was not only completely alien to the Fagan Report. It had been explicitly dismissed as absurd and irrelevant by the Black leaders themselves. This sort of rhetoric was absolutely typical of the distortion of issues that was to continue to be prevalent in South Africa for many years.

As the Government then sought to attract the support of moderate Afrikaners (later termed *verligtes*), who had to be convinced that its policy was something other than a breeding-ground for rebellion, it began to elaborate and to implement the positive side of its policy, which it renamed 'separate (or parallel) development'. With regard to the Blacks in the towns, Dr. Malan appointed the Tomlinson Commission, which sought to substantiate the view that the socio-economic development of the old Native reserves would re-attract the Blacks back from the towns.[52] Hence, this development would effect by economic means the transfer of populations needed to make segregation (in the sense of a partition) a reality. Under Dr. Verwoerd this idea was carried to its 'logical' conclusion with his declaration that these reserves could become politically independent Black states or 'homelands'.[53] Yet the Black population in the towns continued to increase, in response to economic expansion, under the Nationalist Government, despite the prevalence of the same (and even more intensified) Stallardism that had provoked the Fagan Report in the first place. And this is not to mention the anomalies of the Coloureds and the Indians, whose separate political status, after the idea of *even separate* representation in a common legislature had been completely nullified, did not admit the simplicity of a territorial solution. The *verligtheid* of 'separate development' was marked by massive ambiguities and questions, notwithstanding its utopian elegance as a blueprint solution. We could sum up this whole policy as one of cutting off every channel of normal communication between Black and White, and of making not even the parliamentary National Party but the government bureaucracy the sole link between the races. Or else we could call it, as Fagan did, a policy of separation without territorial separation.[54] It was a policy of talking not to but about Blacks.

The effect of this extremist policy on the opposition both in and out of Parliament was that it became fragmented, radicalized, and altogether thrown off centre. It could not get for itself that modicum of distance from government policy to articulate a position which

would meet the issues. Overpowered by the Government's command-
ing rhetoric, it tended to react to this on the ground laid down by the
Government. In the first place this led the United Party to commit a
serious political blunder. Despite having removed the Coloureds in the
Cape from the common roll, the Government still could not command
a popular majority in the 1958 election. But in 1960, when the Government moved to establish South Africa as a republic by a referendum,
the United Party opposed this as yet another attempt by the Government to consolidate the foundations of a sectionalist, extremist regime.
In fact the United Party seriously underestimated the longing of
Afrikaner nationalism for what was its deepest, ultimate political
aspiration. It also lost sight of the fact that by 1960 republican sentiment was no longer that of an extremist or fanatical fringe. Dr. Malan,
who clearly regarded himself as the restorer of Afrikaner nationalism,
did not touch this issue during the six years of his administration. He
knew—perhaps he shared this view himself—that there were many
Afrikaners who, while they had no sentimental attachment to the
British Crown, doubted the wisdom of breaking off the relationship
on prudential grounds. This was not unlike the position of those
French-Canadians today who vote for the Parti Québecois but who
are opposed to independence for Quebec on the grounds that Quebec
'cannot go it alone'. But after Suez, in 1956, this opinion changed in
South Africa. The United Party leadership was in fact advised by some
English-speaking businessmen on the Reef to reconsider the wisdom
of its opposition to the Republic. A delegation of them had gone to see
Dr. Verwoerd privately, offering to support the Republic in exchange
for a new deal on the race question. He expressed interest, but told
them they would have to get the agreement of their party leadership.
The leadership, however, stood fast. Looking at the prospects for the
referendum, it gambled that it might win and discredit the Nationalists.
It could do this, however, only by inciting or by pandering to the anti-
Afrikaner sentiments of the old Unionists or Dominionites in the
United Party, an essentially captive vote. Thus the Government won the
first test of its ability to poll an Afrikaner majority *not* on its race policy
but on this referendum.[55] But it squeaked through to victory with a
majority of only 75,000 out of a total vote cast of 1,600,000, and to get
even this it had lowered the voting age to eighteen. The referendum
accentuated the alienation of Afrikaner nationalism from the United
Party, on an issue which had no material bearing on the regime. As
events were to show, the passions unleashed about the Republic cooled
very quickly. Sentiment in South Africa favouring continued links

with the British Commonwealth evaporated with the intensification of the latter's anti-South Africa stand. The internal political significance of this whole story, however, is that the United Party had thrown away a chance, not to regain power, but to use its political leverage *as an Opposition* to moderate the policy of the regime.

From then on the United Party lost its bearings more and more in the face of the Government's race policy. It could not find a footing upon which to oppose the Government in a politically effective way. Its main point, as Fagan saw it, was that apartheid, or total segregation, was unworkable because of the dependence of the South African economy upon Black labour. But every Nationalist Prime Minister from Dr. Malan onwards publicly admitted the same thing in so many words, namely, that total apartheid was only an 'ideal'.[56] The United Party was prevented by its more liberal elements from projecting as an alternative a policy such as Fagan's, that granted a voice to the urban Blacks in ways which circumvented the 'hot potato' of the common franchise. Nor could it, because of its conservative supporters, look ahead to grab hold of what was potentially sound in the Bantu homelands idea, namely, the restoration of legitimate Black leadership, and disconnect this sound part from the doctrinaire pretensions of Government policy. This would have meant demanding not only the right but the obligation to consult with the homeland leaders in a bi-partisan way about both Black interests and the general welfare of South Africa. The leaders of the United Party, which had a popular majority until the 1961 election, lacked the necessary adroitness to do this because of their illusion, shed only after the 1974 election, that they could still be returned to power. Thus they were not only afraid of sounding too much like the Government, but were prepared to grab at any straw to catch votes, from the right or the left of the latter, from Afrikaners or English.

On the race question, the slogan that the United Party formulated as its 'alternative' to apartheid was 'White leadership with justice over an undivided South Africa'. In essentials this meant a return to the idea of representation of non-Whites in Parliament on separate electoral rolls. This franchise policy was at once subjected to the continual attack of the Nationalists, who argued that it was either the 'thin end of the wedge' or the tokenism of an outmoded colonialist outlook, that would never satisfy the aspirations of non-Whites for political equality.[57] The United Party did indeed recognize the permanence of a settled Black urban community and advocated the expansion of the Black middle class. As for the Black homelands idea, Fagan, it is true,

argued in 1963 against the *verbrokkeling* (fragmentation) of South
Africa, which, together with the abnormality of the situation in the
urban areas, he saw as an invitation to pan-Africanist, anti-White
sentiment.[58] But in presenting themselves as the party 'really' standing
for 'White control', the United Party fell into the trap of pandering to
the most reactionary opinion in South Africa. This was seen not only
in the letter but in the tone of its opposition to further transfers of land
to the Black homelands, which had been promised under the 1936
legislation.* By the late 1950s the United Party had on this issue
assumed the role of the old Purified Nationalists, who had opposed
this legislation at the time as 'spoon-feeding the Kaffir while poor-
Whites lacked land'.[59] The United Party was playing, if in vain, for the
votes of farmers, particularly those on the borders of the Black homelands.

The United Party thus fell between two stools. It began to sound
more and more like a party that was trying to be all things to all men.
Not only was it despised for this by Afrikaner intellectuals, who, if they
broke with the Nationalists, typically found their way not to the United
Party but to the liberal left in South Africa. In addition, the halfway-
house stance of the United Party led to a split within its own ranks by
the liberals, who in 1959 formed the Progressive Party. The triggering
cause of the split was the United Party's opposition to the Government's land policy for Blacks, a policy which had been made law by
the pre-war United Party itself. The Progressives then drew up a
programme for a qualified, non-racial franchise. Between 1961 and
1974, however, they were able to return only one member, though a
very articulate one, from an upper-middle-class constituency of
Johannesburg.†

Beyond the parliamentary Opposition were such organizations as
the African National Congress and South African Indian Congress,
which stood for political integration, and which had been in existence
for years. As soon as the Nationalists were elected, the Government
was on an obvious collision course with these organizations. When the
Government began to implement the legal framework of apartheid,
including the elimination of those existing links for consultation that
it regarded as 'concessions to integration', these organizations then
turned to overt protests, demonstrations, and campaigns of civil
disobedience against such measures as the Pass Laws, the Bantu
Education Act, and the Group Areas Act.[60] There were also riots in

---

* See p. 11.
† Mrs. Helen Suzman, M.P. for Houghton.

the rural areas (for example, Sekukuniland) against the application of
the Bantu Authorities Act. With, as Fagan pointed out, a veritable
vacuum having been created in 'the sphere of interchange of ideas
across the colour line', few Whites even knew the causes of these
disturbances. Their information was limited to newspaper reports of
court proceedings and one or two official statements, which they had
no means of checking.[61]

The Government's response to this civil disturbance was to declare
a state of emergency in 1960 and to ban the protest organizations. A
remnant of their leadership then went underground to plan a guerrilla
movement and sabotage.[62] Against the threat of this the Government
availed itself of extraordinary powers restricting not only freedom of
action but speech. The exercise of these powers only accentuated the
polarization between the two language presses with each blanketly
justifying or condemning whatever the Government did. In the meantime the Government did begin to lay the foundations of machinery for
consultation with non-Whites, but it did so on its terms. The result
was to create and to sustain the most profound suspicion on the part of
the non-Whites as to the intentions of the Government.

From time to time attempts were made to break out of the political
impasse that derived from this polarization, by the formation of a third
party that would restore the centre. The Progressives certainly conceived of themselves as standing in between the extremes of Afrikaner
nationalism on the one hand and Pan-African nationalism on the other.
But as their electoral record showed their stand on the franchise went far
beyond the limit that South African public opinion would carry. Fagan
himself became the leader of the National Union in 1961. This party
sought to carve out a position above the prevailing rhetoric and counter-
rhetoric.[63] But it was too weak to stand by itself and quickly merged
with the United Party, where its point of view never got the upper
hand.

In sum, the overall political effect of the National Party, both on the
race question and on the more strictly ethnic concerns of Afrikaner
nationalism, was to overpower the moderates within the ranks of the
Afrikaners. They stood by as uneasy witnesses to such things as
ambulance apartheid, dislocations of settled communities, interferences
to family life among urban Blacks, and detention without trial, all
imposed with the reiterated assertion that the only alternative was the
suicide of the White man.[64] They knew this was not true and they also
knew that total segregation, in the sense of the removal of Blacks from
the urban areas, was impossible. As I said earlier, the Government

itself admitted this. The action against the Coloured vote in the Cape was also something that troubled moderate Afrikaner opinion. Yet for these moderates there was no politically palatable alternative that was not either too 'liberal' or too 'anti-Afrikaner'. This enabled the government to weld together, in the face of internal and external threats, the moderates and the real extremists in a way that smoothed over the tension between these different segments of Afrikaner opinion. In the next section we shall show that this tension finally broke into the open.

1960–1976: verkramptes, verligtes, *and pragmatists*

The 1974 election did not see any surface change in the fundamental structure of political power in South Africa. It did, however, see a change within the ranks of the parliamentary Opposition. This, together with other things, made it somewhat easier than before to see the character of the political situation that had emerged during the previous decade, and to see what might lie ahead in the immediate future. In the 1961 election the Nationalists got the popular majority of the electorate that they had polled in the referendum of 1960, and which they have continued to maintain at each subsequent election. This was primarily a consolidation of the Afrikaner vote, as is shown by the following survey from 1975:

Table 3: Party preferences according to language, August 1975
(Rapport Poll)

	Afrikaans	English	Total Sample
National Party	83·3	23·4	60·4
Progressive Reform Party	1·0	36·2	14·5
United Party	4·7	24·1	12·2
Herstigte Nasionale Party	3·3	0·5	2·2
Democratic Party	1·3	3·5	2·1
Abstain/No Information	6·5	12·3	8·7

Source: Prof. H. Lever, Dept. of Sociology, Univ. of the Witwatersrand.

Parallel to, though not congruent with, the political ascendancy of the Afrikaner was the socio-economic improvement that the Afrikaners had undergone *vis-à-vis* the English since World War Two. Not only had the poor-Whites, of whom there was still an influx from the *platteland* into the cities until 1951, disappeared as a political class by the 1960s. In addition an expansion of the urban Afrikaner middle class had taken place, connected with the facts in the following table:

*Table 4: Estimated control of selected sectors of
the economy by Afrikaners, 1939 and 1964*

	1939 %	1964 %
Commerce	8	28
Industry	3	10
Finance	5	14
Mining	1	10

Source: S. van Wyk, *Die Afrikaner in die Beroepslewe
van die Stad* (Pretoria, 1968), p. 229. Quoted by David
Welsh in 'Urbanisation and the Solidarity of Afrikaner
Nationalism', *The Journal of Modern African Studies,*
7, 2 (1969), p. 270.

Note: Figures are only very approximate.

As the Government acquired its expanded power-base and in class
respects was no longer so stridently the spokesman for poor-Whites, it
began under Dr. Verwoerd's leadership to shed its populism. It thus
began to move away from both the rhetoric and, in crucial respects,
the substance of the 'Purified Nationalist' stance of earlier days. To
begin with, Dr. Verwoerd was determined to bring the English into
the National Party. He appointed two English-speakers to his Cabinet
and began to woo the English vote, with whom he made a noticeable
breakthrough in the 1966 election. Contributing to this success were
the attacks upon South Africa from abroad, the disorders that had
broken out in the Congo, and the threat of internal insurrection which
the Government, by 1963, had broken. Dr. Verwoerd, in seeking
English support, was well enough placed to enable him easily to project the National Party as the guarantor of domestic order and of the
White man's position in South Africa. And White unity, at least for
Dr. Verwoerd, was something other than Afrikaner *volkseenheid*
(ethnic unity).

On the race question Dr. Verwoerd was also determined to prove
that apartheid or separate development could be stripped of its connotations of inequality or White supremacy in the one sphere where he
saw the possibility of a dramatic gesture. To this end he declared in
Parliament that the Black homelands, which were to be the locus of
Black political rights, could become fully independent, sovereign
states. In 1963 he began to actualize the first phase of homeland
independence, namely, the institution of Bantu [Black] Territorial
Authorities in these areas. But at the same time he had, when Minister

of Bantu Affairs, been addressing himself all along to certain practical exigencies in race relations. He began to implement a social policy for non-Whites of which the two main achievements were a massive slum clearance programme in the *urban areas* and the widespread elimination of illiteracy. He did this in ways which antagonized decent opinion in South Africa. He pushed through legislation which abolished the mission schools, many of which were of high quality and provided a benign contact between White and Black. This legislation also perpetuated a grossly unequal per capita expenditure on education between White and Black pupils, which is a contributing cause of the high rate of attrition among Black pupils at the higher levels. But it is impossible to deny either that expansion did take place in the field of the first four years of primary education. While Dr. Verwoerd held fast to the White-labour policy of the regime, he also self-evidently did not prevent whatever upgrading of Black industrial labour that took place naturally under the boom conditions of the 1960s. Indeed, without this upgrading the boom would not have been possible. In external relations Dr. Verwoerd also began to lay the groundwork in the last years of his life for opening diplomatic relations with neighbouring Black states.

From the point of view of liberal White opinion and Black opinion in South Africa, the independent homelands scheme, when it was first projected, was commonly regarded as an empty gesture, as a fraud intended to delude world opinion. Underlying this judgement, of course, was the fact that economic opportunities for Blacks were to be found, not in the homelands, but in the towns. In fact, as I shall show in the next chapter, economic development in the homelands was blocked by the doctrinaire aspects of Dr. Verwoerd's policy.

I attended the ceremony instituting the Territorial Authority in the Transkei in 1963. This was the first Black reserve to be moved towards independence. Two parties at once emerged, reflecting not so much a real division of interests in the Transkei itself as the ideological issues in the Republic. One party stood for 'separate development', the other for 'multi-racialism'. A Black waiter, who was completely articulate about the politics of the election, ventured to explain to me the difference between the two parties. When he told me that he was for 'multi-racialism', I asked him:

What does multi-racialism really mean to you?
Oh, very simple. The right to work anywhere in South Africa.
Anywhere?
Anywhere. Cape Town, Johannesburg, Durban.

In other words, 'multi-racialism' for the Transkei meant the right to leave it! This is not surprising considering how little there was—and still is—to do there, a conclusion with which the head of the 'separate development' party would be the first to agree.

As for the Government's social policy, there was from the beginning more of a division between liberal White and Black opinion, if not about the facts, certainly about emphasis. Liberal Whites would be inclined to see and to stress the manifest inequality between White and Black. Blacks, on the other hand, while hardly unaware of this inequality, were also inclined to see the difference between the before and after. As one Black put it to me, 'The reason for this is very simple. The shoe pinches on us.' Here are some comments of non-Whites themselves about the social policy:

(*a Coloured man*)
Well, you have to admit the Government has done a lot for us in housing.
(*a Black showing me around one of the Black university colleges*)
As you can see there are two South Africas. There is the South Africa of the Pass Laws and the South Africa of here. When it comes to such things as housing, education, and rural rehabilitation, you have to admit this Government has done more for us than any previous Government. What did the Smuts Government ever do for us?

These remarks were made to me in 1963, on my first visit to South Africa. But note the phrase 'you have to admit', which tells a great deal about the atmosphere in the country. For standing side by side with this liberal White and Black opinion was the politically crucial opinion within the National Party itself. The *verligtes*, who supported the idea of homeland independence and economic development, thought that the homelands were not being developed rapidly enough. They also approved of the slum clearance in the urban areas. One Nationalist put it to me, 'Do you think those townships are temporary?' As events would show, these *verligtes* were also prepared to approve steps by the Government to eliminate the petty apartheid which it had imposed in the beginning. On the other hand there were the *verkramptes* in the National Party who thought the Government was spending too much on the Blacks and who went along with the Bantustan scheme only because they did not think the Government was serious about it. The Government was as much in between two stools as was the United Party. With the enormous prestige and authority that Dr. Verwoerd had acquired during the last years of his life, he was able to keep dissent from both these wings under control, partly by the imposition of iron party discipline, partly by the implementation of policy in a way which fully satisfied neither. But the strength of the *verkramptes* was shown by the fact that, when he announced in Parliament that the homelands could become independent, he had, as I was informed, not dared to clear this with his party's caucus that very morning.

After his death his successor was B. J. Vorster, the man who had been the Minister of Justice under Dr. Verwoerd. He had thus been the very symbol of the tough law-and-order stance of the Nationalist regime. It soon became apparent that Vorster was prepared, not only to continue the *verligte* aspects of Dr. Verwoerd's administration, but to go even further in two racially sensitive matters. He fully normalized relations with Malawi, which appointed a Black ambassador resident in South Africa, and he permitted a rugby tour to take place in South Africa by a national team from New Zealand which included Maoris.

These were only the outermost issues which triggered a split from the right within the National Party which had been brewing ever since the high point of the 1960 referendum. As events were to show, the unity which Afrikaner nationalism was able to muster on the issue of the establishment of the Republic did not exist on the race question. The split took shape in 1969, with the formation of the Herstigte [Re-established] Nasionale Party (H.N.P.)

This party was a resurgence of exactly the same ethnic populism that was behind the split of the Purified Nationalists in 1934. Notwithstanding the guiding presence in this party of some Pretoria intellectuals, one or two poets, and the son of the late General Hertzog, the Herstigtes were mainly ordinary people from both town and country, who had the characteristic fears of the changes in South Africa which they could see taking place, which they neither understood nor liked, and which were being initiated to boot by 'their' party, against all its old professions. The populist character of this revolt, called by some the '*bywoners*' party', was indicated by the way in which its agitation turned now, not on the 'imperialist' gold mines, but on the 'new rich Afrikaner establishment', for whose interests, it was contended, the National Party was now catering. Here is a sample of 1969 Herstigte rhetoric:

[Conservatives] no longer make up the powerful political cultural and religious nucleus that once guided Afrikanerdom as a tightly knit people. And the truth to be faced is that Afrikaner nationalism in present hands is being diluted and will lose its character and identity, unless the drift is halted. . . . The men who have started the National Party on its death walk— and also that of the White nation—are the power elite of liberals and new-rich Afrikaners who, under Mr. Vorster's leadership, have been enabled to gain effective control of the Party.[65]

Exactly like their ancestors, the Purified Nationalists, the Herstigtes turned against the Government, not merely as an 'establishment', but as a 'liberal establishment', which had gone 'soft' on the race question. This meant that the Government was spending too much on the Blacks in the towns, giving away large parts of South Africa to the Blacks by its homelands policy, and dropping the colour bar by receiving Black ambassadors and by allowing Maoris to play rugby (without whom the New Zealand team would not have come). In their agitation they did not hesitate to use racialist epithets which the National Party had for years made unrespectable in its own public deliberations. And, last but not least, the latter was wooing the Afrikaners' old enemy, *die Engelsman*. What they could see was that the Government, which had come into power as the party of *ons volk* (our people), was no longer behaving as 'our' Government. And they saw in this change the foundations of their world, of their way of life, and of everything they stood for, being frittered away at the edges.

According to *Sunday Tribune* (6/15/69), Dr. Beyers attacked Mr. Vorster and the National Party for 'doing too much for the Kaffir'. He said he was not prepared to commit suicide by co-operating with English speakers. According to the *Sunday Times* (6/15/69), Dr. Beyers attacked 'Kaffirs, Jews, Coolies, and English'. He referred to the English as the 'liberal rabble in Johannesburg'. He said that basically there was no longer any difference between the Nationalists and the United Party. 'In fact, we are now the *"Kafferboeties"** and not the United Party.'

Dr. Beyers added: 'Our children will not only have to play with the children of Black diplomats, they will also have to associate with the Black Portuguese. Our ancestors called these Portuguese "sea Kaffirs".' He said that in some respects, we were worse than the Communists. What they did for the 'Kaffirs' had an ulterior motive. 'We are apparently doing it for love. The worst of all is the enhanced status which the "Kaffir" has these days.' In all the newspapers you read of 'Miss Kaffir', 'Mr. Kaffir', or 'Mrs. Maid'.[66]

The Nationalist leaders, of course, knew that much of the feeling underlying this split from the right was shared throughout the ranks of the Nationalist electorate. How many Nationalist voters really supported the policy of sovereign independence for the Black homelands? I mentioned earlier that when Dr. Verwoerd first dropped this idea like a small bombshell, he had not even dared to clear it with his caucus. Now, faced with an attack from the right, which was potentially far more than a mere splinter, the Government responded to this danger to party unity and party loyalty with all the political weapons

* A derogatory term: literally 'Kaffir-lovers'.

at its disposal. It called a general election a year in advance (1970). It did not hesitate to use the security police to crack down on smear letters from Herstigte sources, or even to use hooligan tactics to break up Herstigte campaign meetings. It did this to the crocodile tears of the English-speaking press, which had no idea what a *broedertwis* (brother's quarrel) was going on or what it meant.[67] For a variety of reasons the English in this election returned to their traditional home in the United Party.[68] Maladministration and a drop in share prices played a role. But the two political reasons were that extra-parliamentary opposition had been virtually eliminated by 1970, and that Vorster had not yet acquired the confidence of English-speaking voters in the way that Dr. Verwoerd had done. The United Party gained 8 seats in this election, making its first recovery since 1948. The Herstigtes, on the other hand, were completely routed at the polls. They ran 78 candidates and most of them lost their deposits. The 4 H.N.P. members, who had defected from the National Party and who held seats in Parliament, were all defeated. But this poor showing was due to the fact that many Nationalist voters who were in sympathy with the Herstigte or *verkrampte* standpoint could not bring themselves to vote against their old party. Party loyalty in South Africa is always a powerful factor. This is true above all for the National Party, which is closely intertwined with the Dutch Reformed Church and the Afrikaner community. If *verkrampte* Nationalists were unhappy with the 'Afrikaner liberal establishment', they did not express their dissatisfaction by voting for the United Party, which these people regarded as anti-Afrikaner. They abstained instead.

If the split of the Herstigtes from the National Party was only the most visible part of the iceberg, we may readily imagine the tensions at work in the local Nationalist constituencies. Let me illustrate this by a few remarks about one man. These give an indication of what was going on in the National Party in the years between 1970 and 1974.

This man, when I interviewed him in 1970, was the mayor of a small Transvaal town. He was then 45 years of age. A friend of mine thought it would be interesting for me to meet him, as he was an outspoken admirer of Vorster's, yet had got into trouble with the 'old guard' of the National Party branch in his town who were out to 'get him'. My friend also told me that as a youth during the war the mayor had been a fervent admirer of the O.B., but in recent years had rediscovered Smuts, and was keenly reading biographies about him.

I went to see him, now a successful businessman, and was received very cordially. He told me that he was, indeed, an admirer of Vorster's and approved very much of what the Government was doing for the Blacks. I began the interview by asking him to recall how he felt when he heard that his party had won in 1948:

I remember that day very well. It was a wonderful feeling. I felt proud. For the first time in my life we Afrikaners did not have to be ashamed.

I then asked him what apartheid meant to him at that time:

No equal rights for Bantu.
  What about the Coloureds?
Them too.

I eventually turned the interview to the friction between him and the Nationalist 'old guard'. He then told me the following. A Black businessman in the township, whom he had known for years, had come to him asking for a trading licence to open up a second business. But government policy was that Blacks should be limited to one trading licence in the townships, opening up second businesses only in the homelands. The Black businessman had said to him, 'Look man, I've got five children to educate and my back is up against the wall.' The mayor then gave him the second trading licence. The 'old guard' were using the fact that he had in this case deviated from government policy as a pretext to depose him from office. Such faction-fighting became part of the everyday atmosphere within the National Party. The Broederbond also became divided in two. Now it would be rash to conclude that the tension between this man's simple practical decency and prevailing policy meant that he was anything less than one hundred per cent Nationalist. It would be equally rash, however, to conclude that the *verkramptheid* of the old guard was so doctrinally pure that they really gave a fig about whether the Black did or did not have a second dry-cleaning shop. What is clear, however, is that by 1970 the Government had got itself into a position where its own words could be used by its own supporters to embarrass it. And, facing an Opposition which was prepared to do exactly the same thing, if with different intentions, the Government was really in between, not two stools, but two pairs of stools. It is no accident that South African politics became covered by rhetorical balloons. Every time the Government quietly made a modification of its policy which then became publicly known, it had to deny blatantly that any fundamental change in policy had been made at all. This was true even when there was an obvious deviation, as in the policy on racially mixed sports, which, however much it may have been minimized outside South Africa, was not minimized by the Herstigtes. Under these circumstances it is under-

standable that the Government had the strongest inducement to get
a mandate, not for its rhetorically projected policy of separate development, which it had not the slightest intention of changing, but rather
to apply the latter how it wanted. To get such a mandate, however,
meant putting down, in a test of electoral strength, not only the
Herstigtes, but the United Party as well. And the opportunity to do
precisely this fell into the hands of the Prime Minister in the period
immediately preceding the April 1974 election.

   This election was called a year in advance, as in 1970, when the
timing was intended to confound the Herstigtes. In 1974, however, the
Government saw that the United Party was openly divided, after a
power struggle had broken out in 1973 between the national leadership
and the Representatives of the Witwatersrand constituencies. The
triggering cause of this disunity was a civil liberties question. The
national leadership of the United Party had agreed to participate in a
bi-partisan parliamentary commission (the Schlebusch Commission)
to investigate certain anti-apartheid organizations. The United Party
could have demanded a voice in the bi-partisan formation of race
policy as the terms for participating in this Commission, but failed to
do so. In the aftermath of the investigation certain individuals were
banned, which conflicted with official United Party policy about the
use of judicial rather than discretionary executive authority in dealing
with alleged subversives. The urban liberals in the Witwatersrand then
revolted. This came to a head in a struggle for the leadership of the
Transvaal branch of the party, in which the man who had been the
provincial leader for years and who was a close associate of the national
leader of the party was defeated. (He subsequently resigned from the
United Party, crossed the floor, and is now a member of the Cabinet.)
After the date of the election had been announced there was further
in-fighting about the nominations.

   The Nationalists, campaigning on the line that they were the only
people who could be trusted to run the country, won the election,
increasing their popular vote over their 1970 result, though not returning to the peak they achieved in 1966. With the help of a new delimita-
tion, which increased the size of the House by 5, the Nationalists also
gained 6 seats, giving them a strength of 123 out of a total of 171. Here
too, however, they did not quite return to their 1966 peak of 126 seats.
The Herstigtes, who refused even to supply the English press with any
details of their policy, fielded candidates who, once again, were all
defeated. By the time of the election the Nationalist victory was
regarded as such a foregone conclusion that the only politically open

question was the performance of the United Party. In the event the
latter lost 4 seats to the Nationalists and 5 to the Progressives, who,
from the time they first stood as a party in 1961, had been able to
return only one member from an upper-middle-class constituency of
Johannesburg. (They had come close to winning a second seat from a
similar Cape Town constituency in the 1970 election, which they, in
fact, won in the 1974 election.) There was also a fifth party that
emerged in this election, the Democratic Party, led by Mr. Theo
Gerdener, a former minister in the Nationalist Government. Thi-
party espoused a legalistic but *verligte* line, standing for the indepens
dence and development of the Black homelands, and, in addition, a
new definition of urban Blacks by the proclamation of urban homelands. The last point was a deviation from Nationalist policy, which
still held fast to its definition of the urban areas as White areas in which
Blacks could not obtain freehold rights. This party was really the
personal candidacy of Gerdener, who had been a popular administrator
of Natal and who, in this election, was just one of four candidates
standing for Parliament in Pietermaritzburg North, a Natal constituency. Here are the results of the parliamentary and provincial
council elections which took place simultaneously, for the first time
in a general election:

Table 5: Parliamentary and provincial council election
results, Pietermaritzburg North, 1974

Party	Parliamentary	Provincial
United	3 825	4 077
Democratic	3 431	1 820
National	2 570	2 584
Progressive	96	1 443

As can be seen from these results, Gerdener, the Democratic
parliamentary candidate, not only came within 394 votes of winning,
but out-polled the Nationalist. He did this, however, with the whole-
hearted support of Progressives, who were determined to show that
the United Party was ineffective as an Opposition.

The drift away from the United Party, to the Nationalists on the
one hand, and to the Progressives on the other, was the most massive
change in the 1974 election. In the absence of careful interviews with
party switchers, one cannot say with finality what this change meant.
But there are clues available, not only from a small number of existing

interviews, but also from the way the issues presented themselves in the campaign. To begin with there was the civil liberties issue discussed above, which sharply divided the national leadership of the United Party from the urban liberals. It was largely because of his implication in this issue that one of the leaders of the United Party lost his seat to a Progressive in Orange Grove, a Johannesburg constituency.

Then there was the party's standpoint on race policy. The United Party, while no longer sounding its old line of 'White control over an undivided South Africa' with quite the same explicitness, still stood opposed in its official pronouncements to sovereign independence for the homelands, on the old grounds that this would lead to the creation of potentially Communist states on the borders of South Africa. Now for the Herstigtes to attack the homeland policy as well as every other movement towards equality for the non-Whites, economic or political, was one thing. But for a party which aspired and claimed to be a centre, to attack the National Party of South Africa for being unmindful of the danger of Communism, was to lose credibility with its own adherents. This was all the more so in view of the fact that the Black leaders who came into office under the homelands policy, which the Government began to push more rapidly after 1970, all proved to be, however articulate their criticism of the racial situation in South Africa, moderates. What is more they had become recognized by both Black and White alike as legitimate Black spokesmen in South Africa. For the United Party to campaign against independence when most of the Black leaders themselves questioned it was to put itself into a politically foolish posture. The United Party could in theory have campaigned on Fagan's policy of effective consultation on a bi-partisan basis with both the permanently urbanized Blacks, recognized as such, *and* the leaders of the Black homelands, whether sovereignly independent or not, leaving it open to them to decide about this aspect of their future. This, the key element in racial policy, was and still is the only ground, both of effective opposition to the Government, and also of any restored centre coalition. Blocking this flexibility, however, was the conception the national leadership of the United Party had of itself as an 'alternative' government that was on the way back to power. Hence, it was seduced into the fantastic position of opposing the Government's rhetoric with another 'blueprint'. This time the policy put forth as the 'alternative' to the Government's policy was called the 'federal plan', a modification of an earlier 'race federation' idea of the 1950s. This conceived of the future government of South Africa as a confederation of nations, in which all the racial groups would have their own parliaments to control their own affairs, with a federal assembly overarching them all, but in a framework in which the White Parliament would control the purse-strings. The man in the street could not even understand—and I am sure was hardly cognizant of— its complicated legalistic details. At any Nationalist rally, the applause for the speaker warning how the federal assembly would become Blacker and Blacker and Blacker, would make it easy to tell how public opinion in South Africa (to whom the United Party was presenting the federal plan as a means of averting the danger of Communism) would react to this plan, to the extent that it took it seriously at all. More than this, however, the United Party fell into the trap of virtually ignoring, not only the existence of the homeland leaders, who certainly were not consulted about the 'federal plan', but also the whole structure of relationships which had evolved between them and the Government, which no political party in South Africa could repudiate.

The Progressives, on the other hand, did not in the 1974 election present themselves frontally as the party with an 'alternative blue-print'. Their main themes were 'change' and 'more effective opposition'. The Progressives did not repudiate their old standpoint of the common (qualified) franchise for the Coloureds, Indians, and urban Blacks. Progressive candidates who were elected told me that in their campaigning they were sharply queried about their stand on this, which still is politically as much the 'impossible issue' as ever. But in accepting the idea of Black homelands, which they too had previously opposed, the Progressives found themselves somewhat closer to the centre of South African public opinion than they had ever been before.

In addition to this they politicked well. They selected candidates of recognized calibre who among other things were fully bilingual and campaigned in both languages. (So did the Prime Minister when he spoke in Johannesburg.) They made use of good old Nationalist techniques of saturation campaigning at the grass-roots, including such things as *huisbesoek* (house visits). And they did not contest seats where a *verligte* United Party candidate ran against a Nationalist in a two-way race. Six weeks after the general election the Progressives followed up their gains with another by-election win in Pinelands, a Cape Town constituency, which had been a United Party safe seat. This victory, though very marginal, discredited the United Party establishment even more than did the general election. For they were still in-fighting with the reformists about the losses in the general election at the time of the by-election. Political commentators at once calculated that on the basis of their performance in Pinelands, there were 20 of the 41

United Party seats that were within the grasp of the Progressive Party.

All this intensified the acrimony of the struggle within the United Party between the national leadership and the urban-based reformists. And indeed, within the year, the reformists split from the United Party, then subsequently merged with the Progressives to form the Progressive-Reformist Party. This is essentially a realignment of the urban liberal vote. Whether it had found itself on the left wing of the United Party (which was the original home of the Progressives) or in the Progressive Party, it consists of the same people. As shown by Table 3, they are predominantly English-speaking. As not shown by this table, they are significantly enough Jewish to be noticeable as such in South African politics. Houghton, in Johannesburg, which was the sole Progressive seat until the 1974 election, and which the Nationalists thus far do not even contest, has a large Jewish population. So does Sea Point in Cape Town. While this urban liberal force in South Africa, for whom Jan Hofmeyr was a hero, has always had Afrikaners in key positions of leadership and would like to attract more, it remains predominantly English-speaking. It is also upper-middle class and is estranged from the White (that is, Afrikaner) working class in the same way as is its counterpart in the United States from the White 'ethnics'. These ethnic and class factors, in addition to the policy stance, thus circumscribe the politically possible expansion of this force.

The immediate aftermath of the 1974 election, in which the Nationalists were not simply returned to power but returned in the face of a further fragmentation of the official Opposition, is that the Government, or to be more precise, the Prime Minister emerged with a solid base of power that no South African prime minister had ever before possessed. This placed extraordinary initiative to act and to lead within his hands, which he began to display, first of all, in diplomatic initiatives with both neighbouring and more distant African states. The Government began to assert, more vocally than ever before, that South Africa was part of Africa. It began to talk, more vocally than ever before, of *détente* and dialogue with Black Africa. The Prime Minister made personal visits to a few Western-oriented African countries, which were a break-through in this respect. South African Airways, which had been shut out of Central Africa for years, now lands in the Ivory Coast. With a primary interest in a stable situation in Southern Africa, he made clear South Africa's interest in a constitutional settlement between Black and White in Rhodesia, though stressing in his public pronouncements that a real settlement there would only take place from within. He also publicly reaffirmed South Africa's commitment to

3

independence for South West Africa, first excluding, latterly agreeing to admit SWAPO to the negotiation. When, within days of the election, the revolution in Portugal took place, with the pronouncement that power in Mozambique would be transferred to FRELIMO, Mr. Vorster made the cool announcement that South Africa did not care what the colour of the government in Mozambique was so long as it was stable. This moderate stance was reciprocated by the FRELIMO leader on his accession to power in June 1975. Needless to say the disappearance of the Portuguese 'shield', the emergence of Marxist governments in Mozambique and Angola after the entry of Cuban troops, and the build-up of guerrilla pressure based in Mozambique upon Rhodesia created a new situation with international repercussions. The Government terminated its short-lived military intervention in Angola in support of the anti-M.P.L.A. forces. But it has not relaxed in its posture as a guardian of South Africa's security against any form of violent change, from within or from without.

Some changes were also made in the internal situation, where the Government now openly says that it must eliminate 'discrimination'. I shall describe the key features of the dynamics of the internal situation in detail in the next two chapters. It suffices to say for the moment that these changes, however welcomed by the *pars maior et sanior* of public opinion, are not nor are regarded within South Africa as anything comparable in scope to the foreign initiatives or to what is required for a genuine settlement of the race problem in South Africa. Even the Government-supporting press will admit this. But the realistic or constitutional recognition of this fact is also part of the new situation in South Africa.

The impact of this new situation upon the internal party structure of South Africa can be seen most clearly in the by-elections which took place in the two years after the 1974 general election. In fact, they show the need for realignment within the party structure more clearly than did the general election itself. The four most significant by-elections are illustrated by Table 6. The first three of these constituencies were all Afrikaner Nationalist strongholds. Gezina and Middelburg are rural or small-town constituencies in the Transvaal; Alberton is an urban constituency adjacent to Johannesburg. In all three the H.N.P. made gains relative to the other parties, and in both Middelburg and Alberton it outpolled the United Party. In all three it campaigned on the line of 'anti-*détente*', 'no dilution of apartheid', and support for the Whites in Rhodesia. The results thus show, at the very least, that the extreme right of the political spectrum in South Africa, while still unable

Table 6: Some recent by-election results, 1975–6

Gezina

Party	25 June 1975	1974 General Election	1970 General Election
National	5 660	7 624	7 431
H.N.P.	1 505	1 100	1 380
Poll	49.0%		

Middelburg

Party	25 June 1975	1974 General Election	1970 General Election
National	4 774	5 238	6 074
H.N.P.	2 353	1 675	833
United	1 662	2 066	2 874
Poll	64·0%		

Alberton

Party	31 March 1976	1974 General Election	1970 General Election
National	6 801	7 662	7 804
H.N.P.	1 004	613	450
United	952	1 719	2 616
Poll	58·6%		

Durban North

Party	5 May 1976	1974 and 1970 General Elections	1966 General Election
Progressive-Reformist	4 243		879
United	3 919	Unopposed	6 169
National	3 139		2 830
Independent	95		159
Poll	75·97%		

to elect a candidate or even avoid losing its deposit, is not extinguished.

Durban North, on the other hand, was a United Party stronghold, in fact an unopposed seat since 1966. Its social complexion is altogether different from the other three, being 92% English-speaking. With the Progressive-Reformist win, the movement in this by-election was evidently in the opposite direction. (The Independent candidate campaigned on a pro-Rhodesia line similar to that of the H.N.P.) One must note, however, the performance of the Nationalist candidate, an English-speaking Senator. He improved upon the performance of the Nationalists in the 1966 election, when Dr. Verwoerd first decided to break into the English-speaking bastion of Natal.

As to whether these developments portend a new 'polarization' or a new 'centralization' (or perhaps both), let us leave for the moment predictions or guesses about party performance in future elections to restate as clearly as possible what the political problem in South Africa is. As indicated at the outset of this chapter one must perceive this from within the practical perspective of the politicians in that society. A grasp of the problem so seen is a reasonable guide to what the politicians have to face up to and to the predictions and guesses that they themselves will be making in the course of the events they shape. And this course can be affected by chance events that no one, practically speaking, expects either to happen at all or to happen when they do. The social scientist, to be sure, must aspire to a perspective which is more comprehensive than that of any of the politicians in that society. The latter, certainly in their public statements, necessarily engage in partisan exaggeration or oversimplification that reflects the force of the regnant prejudices of the day. But, to make sense, the perspective of the social scientist must be only a step forward from the perspective of the politicians and must look in the same direction. This is axiomatic if one wants to understand practice or action rather than reduce it to a level of explanation where the phenomena disappear.[69]

From this practical perspective the fundamental problem or what Hertzog called '*die groot* [great] *probleem vir Suid Afrika*', is, as everyone knows, a just relationship between White and Black.[70] This problem, which used to be called 'the Native question' around 1900, may be defined as how to give the non-Whites an effective voice in the Government in a way which preserves and indeed fortifies the constitutional character of the regime. This presupposes not simply political change, in a narrow, legalistic sense, but also those socio-economic changes which affect the heart of what democratic equality in modern times is all about. These would constitute a change towards equality of what Tocqueville called '*l'état social*'.

Though this is the fundamental problem, however, it has not been the most politically urgent problem under discussion in this initial chapter. The problem which can rightfully claim this priority since the formation of Union has been the emergence of an effective government, or the bringing into being of a stable majority among those who constitutionally had the say in South Africa, namely, the Whites, or the Afrikaners and the English. The reason why this has been the most urgent consideration is the quintessence of simplicity. Only such a government could deal in an adequate manner with the fundamental problem. The fact that elected governments are elected does not make them *eo ipso* any the less governments than monarchies or aristocracies in having to address themselves to difficult problems.[71] Just as monarchies were weakened by a disputed succession, so can democracies be weakened—indeed, paralysed—by a precarious and shifting majority, as the experience of this century amply confirms.

This dictum of practical common sense, so stated, must, however, be distinguished from a doctrinaire and self-serving version of it which has played a considerable role in public discussion of the race problem in South Africa, as it did in the American South around the turn of the century. This version is something like the following. If only the Whites were not divided by the question of the Black franchise, or if the Blacks were not a pawn in White politics, then the Whites could unite and treat the Blacks justly. This was the rhetorical justification for taking first the Blacks and then the Coloureds off the common electoral roll in the Cape, with the virtual presumption that this was being done for the benefit of the non-Whites. Exactly the same rhetoric was heard in the disfranchising conventions in the American South. From this justification it is a short step to the view that disunity among the Whites on this issue is suicidal, disloyal, subversive. But this is equine logic. The fundamental socio-political fact is that if the Whites are divided about things that concern themselves, this division will encompass the race problem and the Blacks will indeed become a pawn to their own disadvantage.

In the light of these remarks I have asserted the thesis in this chapter that an effective majority or centre coalition came into being in South Africa with the formation of the United Party. Its formation, which was a *toenadering* (approchement) between 'Boer' and 'Briton', was an acknowledgement by Afrikaner nationalism that the outstanding grievances created by the injustice of the South African War had been resolved. One should not forget, however, the role which the chance factor, namely, the Depression, played in facilitating the formation of the coalition at the given historical moment. The United Party then moved to settle the 'Native question'. The settlement it thought it brought about, namely, the policy of 'segregation', was seen by people far in advance of prevalent public opinion to be out of date when it was enacted.[72] Smuts himself came to describe it fairly quickly as an 'unsettlement'. The United Party would thus have had to move to make the needed changes in race policy, along the lines of the Report of the Fagan Commission, to adjust to the fact of a permanent dependence of the South African economy upon urban Black labour. Chance factors, which had nothing to do with the race problem, prevented this from taking place. First they caused the break-up of the coalition between Afrikaners and English. Second, they prevented it from taking shape again quickly enough to clip the wings of the extremist wing of Afrikaner nationalism that remained outside this coalition at its beginning.

This extremist wing of Afrikaner nationalism, aided and abetted in its political career by these chance factors, then came to power. It did so, however, as a minority which, we are inclined to say, was never intended to be any more than an opposition ethnic pressure group. When it found itself, so to speak, in office, it behaved like any other political party in comparable circumstances. It set about transforming itself into a majority party. Given its electorate, however, it could only proceed to do this by accentuating all those cleavages—between Afrikaner and English and between White and non-White—that were the bases of its existence as an opposition ethnic party. At the root of all its calculations was the politico-demographic fact that the Afrikaners were 60% of the White population. Still, the acquisition of an Afrikaner ethnic electoral majority, which it eventually brought about in 1961, may well be seen before the fact not as inevitable but as amazing.

Today the Nationalist Government is not only a majority government but is or seems to be the most stable government in the West. No other party has been continuously longer in office. And no other party in South Africa can constitutionally depose it. To be sure, it is possible to say that a majority of the whole South African population does not choose this Government. But this does not gainsay, either, the change which has occurred and which can take place among those constitutionally entitled to choose it. Yet for all the preponderance of its parliamentary strength and power, the Government is not a true centre. This means, to recall what was said earlier, a government which can bind together not simply *a* majority but rather *that* majority which it needs to support a moderate course of action. This in turn means a policy which addresses itself to the most urgent problems of the day. As Fagan saw, this would be one which resolved the situation of the urban Blacks, the Coloureds, and the Indians in a way that Whites felt did not threaten their security and freedom. Only such a policy could carry White opinion with it in a constitutional way. That such a centre exists and is not simply a figment of my or anyone else's imagination is easily seen by two facts. The first is the Government's own accommodation to the exigencies of reality, sense, and decency. The second is not merely the acquiescence but the approval of the preponderant part of White public opinion for these changes; I am referring among other things to those voices within the National Party itself which have been speaking out for the restoration of the Coloureds to the common electoral roll. That the Government cannot bind up this centre is also easily seen by the contortions, gyrations, and rhetorical obfuscations in its policy as it moves to do the right thing.

Given the way in which this Government came to and rose in power, with its polarized electorate, all this sociologically is not surprising. One must not forget that any time someone in the Government deviates from Nationalist orthodoxy to move towards a dictate of common sense, he may find himself facing the charge that he is betraying his people. Thus what is really surprising is the good the Government has been able to achieve within the constrictions of its sectionalized power-base. The move, for example, on the part of the Government to create not so much independent Black homelands as rather independent Black leadership was a move towards Black equality, perhaps the only one possible within the boundaries of National Party opinion at the time. This proved at any rate to be the means by which Dr. Verwoerd publicly discredited and silenced the populist-racialist line of his predecessor, that apartheid meant '*Witbaasskap*' (White control), the outlook which then resurfaced in the H.N.P. However much the territorial aspect of this policy was presented as a 'solution' to the status of the Blacks in the towns, it was not so much a solution as a suspension of a solution.

In the meantime the opposition party created by this polarization also could not bind up the centre. The United Party could not do this because it had alienated Afrikaner nationalism as an ethnic force, and could never recapture its allegiance. The United Party's divagations on the issue of the general franchise were another political liability in trying to reach the centre, which applies *a fortiori* to the Progressives and the former Liberal Party. But on its urban policy, the United Party was absolutely sound throughout its long years in opposition. It was prepared to implement the recommendations of the Fagan Commission. And to recall what was said earlier, the split of the Progressives was not about the urban policy of the United Party but about the *verkrampte* standpoint it took in 1959 on rural policy. In this respect, the Progressives were actually closer to the *verligte* Nationalists than they were to the *verkrampte* Natalians in the United Party.

What follows may thus seem to be axiomatic. This is that it is impossible for any government in South Africa to rise to the exigencies it has to face without a restoration of a centre coalition between the moderate segments of English and Afrikaner nationalist opinion. (This coalition, within the normal framework of the parliamentary structure, would at once be the basis of a broader coalition, between Whites, Coloureds, Blacks, and Indians, within the 'exceptional' framework needed to give them a voice in the Government.) This is as true today as it was at the time of the Hertzog-Smuts Fusion, as well as of that lost chance between Smuts and Havenga. Since such coalitions are not simply engineered in order to fulfil the abstract 'functional imperatives of a political system', but come into being when they do by the impingement of chance factors, I limit myself here to a discussion of those factors which belong to the domain of reason rather than that of chance.

The key point to emphasize is that such a coalition must not be confused with a mere amalgamation of the National and the United Parties as they exist at the moment. To precipitate a restoration of the centre requires a restructuring of policy to comprehend both the rural and urban poles of the racial situation as a whole, in a way which puts the most urgent problems facing South African society in their true order of priority. This means, first and foremost, facing up to the unresolved problem of the permanently settled Blacks in the towns, and disconnecting it from the homeland solution which permitted the tail to wag the dog. In order for this restructuring to take place (we could say in an abstract way) each party would have to get rid of its extremes. In fact it is the National Party by virtue of its power which would have to make the first move. Given the division within the National Party, however, what is more significant is the expansion of the authority of the Prime Minister that has taken place. In mid-1976, Vorster, having acquired the status of a president, became the only person in the country capable of binding up the centre so as to transcend not merely party but race. For over a year the English press had been urging him to stop looking over his shoulder at the right wing of his party; and the Black press took to saying the same thing.

In making clear the policy which would constitute the basis of this centre, I can, at the risk of only minor oversimplification, put it as follows. What divides the common-sense centre of Afrikaner Nationalist voters from the doctrinaire fanatics who have propounded racial policy since Dr. Verwoerd's entry into the Government is the issue of the permanence of the urbanized Black labour force. This coloured the debate about freehold home-ownership. In fact the ordinary Nationalist voter, to whom the Black townships are 'native locations' that always were there and always will be, was probably unaware of the fact that the Blacks could not own their houses in freehold, until the Afrikaner press pointed this out in the aftermath of the Soweto* riots. The law was changed in August 1976. For English-speaking voters, on the other hand, freehold for urban Blacks has never been an issue since 1948. The issue that divides them that is relevant in the present context is the question how to deal with anti-constitutional subversion. In South Africa as elsewhere constitutional liberal opinion is, to put it mildly, uneasy about the tension between the need to combat subversion and the civil rights of individuals. In South Africa this dilemma has been immeasurably complicated by the doctrinaire race policy propounded by a government which, having for so many years cut off effective consultation between itself and moderate non-White leaders, undermined their status and authority. Whatever one's political standpoint, one should not find it difficult to see that this is precisely the soil in which agitators propounding familiar revolutionary rhetoric about total liberation through violent change can not merely arise—because they are there whether one likes it or not—but can flourish by discrediting the moderates as 'Uncle Toms' who by constitutional means can achieve nothing. Yet as repugnant as the English-speaking voter may find those doctrinaire aspects of the race policy that from 1948 to now have been fully reported by the English-speaking press, the stance of most English-speaking voters on organized subversion is no different from that of the Afrikaner voters. Thus it is easy to see that a policy which united a sobriety about the racial situation with a firm defence against uncon-stitutional change, would unite the preponderant part of White opinion. It would also have the support of the preponderant part of non-White opinion. This was seen in the reaction of ordinary Black workers to the wanton lawlessness triggered in the Soweto riots by the initial demonstration against a genuine grievance. It is equally evident that a mere pandering to a law-and-order White backlash would create a polarization between White and non-White of a magnitude that has never before been experienced. This brings the discussion back to the domain of chance.

In this chapter I have concentrated upon what in South Africa is oddly called 'White politics', which describes Whites talking mainly about Blacks. In the next chapter I shall examine the socio-economic reality that affects the Blacks. There is bound to be repetition of a number of the same facts. But there is no other way of analysing the macro-sociological or political problem in an orderly fashion.

* An acronym of 'South West Township'.

II

Economics and Politics

The rise of the segregation policy

As I indicated in the previous chapter, terms such as 'segregation' arose and acquired their precise meaning in specific economic and even military contexts. Thus to postulate a historical continuity in policy in a way which abstracts from these different contexts may be misleading. In the early history of South Africa, as in the United States and New Zealand, contact between the native tribes and the European settlers moving out from their original settlements, resulted in military conflict. This gave rise to the idea, favoured by central administrations, of a frontier within which White settlement was to be contained, as a basis of order and peace. Since the central administrations were too weak to defend the frontier adequately, it kept breaking down in a chronic series of wars until the same end result was reached, at about the same time as in the countries with parallel situations. This was conquest of the native tribes and the unification of the whole under White hegemony.

In South Africa, unlike the United States, the Whites entered into economic relations with the native population. Unlike the American Indians, the Blacks in South Africa became the labour supply on extensive landholdings, which were cut off from a market and which, as Frankel has pointed out, acquired the function of opening up a continent to European settlement.[1] Because of this economic interdependence and also because of their recent memory of military conflict, the White farmers were antagonistic to the idea of segregated reserves, except as places to 'locate' Blacks who were surplus to their labour requirements.[2] The reserve, as a protection for native landholdings which were rendered legally inalienable, was an institution of the imperial administration, just as in the United States it was of the federal government versus local interests. Reitz, the President of the Free

State, in a polemic against Shepstone's reserve policy in the British colony of Natal, attacked the reserves as an abomination, 'the prop of despotic chieftainship', and of a social system which permitted the enslavement of women by men 'who were too proud to work but not too proud to steal'.[3] In the Free State reserves hardly took shape at all.[4] Even in Natal, what came to be called Shepstone's policy was not unmindful either of military considerations or of the potential labour needs of the White farmers, as seen by the fragmented pattern of the reserves.[5] It must be pointed out, however, that for a time Shepstone's policy had the effect of reducing the incentive of Blacks to leave the reserves to seek work. It is for this reason that Indians were brought over to work the sugar plantations in Natal.[6]

Within a generation, this antagonism to the idea of reserves, which Reitz contended was prevalent public opinion throughout the whole of South Africa, changed into the new cry of 'Send them back' (to the reserves) which represented a very different view of this discredited institution.[7] What brought about the change? Very simply, urbanization. In this respect it may be of interest to examine briefly the recommendations of the *Report of the South African Native Affairs Commission 1903–1905*. This Commission was appointed before the Union, in anticipation of the coming federation, to lay down a uniform native policy for the whole country. Its Report is a documentation of the fact that South Africa was changing from a fundamentally agricultural society, in which the main political accent of native policy was the demand by White farmers for protection against squatting, into an industrial society; but one which, as events were to prove, the country was not yet prepared to accept. The Report of this Commission underlay the Natives Land Act of 1913, which segregated or apportioned land-ownership on a racial basis in the rural areas. Hence, it has been argued with care by Tatz that this Report was the beginning point of what culminated first in 'segregation' and then in 'apartheid'.[8]

In developing his thesis, Tatz understandably calls attention to the following points. In the first place the Commission recommended the containment of the Black population in the rural areas to clearly demarcated reserves or locations, the boundaries of which would have to be permanently fixed.[9] In line with this it recommended that the practice of squatting on Crown lands and European farms be checked.[10] It further recommended, though with the dissent of one of its members, to terminate the right of Blacks and also Whites to buy land in mixed areas, on the grounds that this would lead to conflict.[11] And finally it argued against the extension of the non-racial franchise in the Cape to the numerically superior Black population and in favour of a separate mode of representation for this population.[12] Here one sees what seems to be not only the 'origin of segregation', but a policy of driving Blacks off the land to supply cheap labour for the mines.

When one looks at the urban provisions of the *Report*, however, one is at once confronted with certain recommendations which not only do not 'fit' with this thesis but which were completely at variance with contemporary Nationalist policy. These included: (1) the right of Blacks to buy freehold property in the urban locations and to make whatever improvements to their property they wished; (2) the encouragement of Blacks to live with their families near their places of employment to eliminate the prime cause of their being discontinuous workers; (3) the encouragement of a higher standard of living among Blacks 'by support given to education with a view to increase their efficiency and wants'; (4) the encouragement of industrial and manual training in schools; and (5) the abolition of obstructions to travel among Blacks such as taxes upon passes.[13]

It is, in fact, only in the light of these urban recommendations that one can see the real thrust and intention of this Report. The Commissioners saw that South Africa had experienced an unusually rapid entry into the industrial age. Citing the findings of the earlier Transvaal Labour Commission of 1903, they noted that this had created a demand for Black labour to meet the requirements of agriculture, mining, and other industries, which 'was in excess of the supply, and that the demand would in all probability increase'.[14] Among the reasons they adduced for this was:

The inexpensiveness of their living, the limited nature of their wants, and the comparative absence of incentive to labour.[15]

Among the causes of this, in turn, was the traditional Black way of life as herdsmen and small cultivators, the absence of a class accustomed to and dependent upon continuous daily labour, and—what may seem almost unbelievable today—the possession of 'easy access to the land'.[16] Squatting, it is true, was a chronic cause of complaint by progressive White farmers. It was also, however, encouraged by land speculators engaging in what was called in South Africa 'Kaffir farming'.

What may seem paradoxical at first sight but what the Commissioners saw with unusual clarity is that the causes of the shortage of Black labour were the selfsame causes of its 'cheapness'. Hence, change in the former would imply change in the latter, that is, the rise of settled communities of Black workers with the skills and wants of civilized labour. The Commissioners may have erred, as Dr. Brookes contended, in being myopic about the poor-White problem and the agitation that would break forth about this.[17] But nothing that has happened in the South African economy from 1900 to the present has in any way invalidated the prediction of the Commissioners that the 'demand for Black labour would increase'. As for the reserves, the Commissioners saw that these were the loci, though not exclusively, of communal, tribal tenure in land, and that this was not only incompatible with modern life but was something under which energetic Blacks themselves had begun to chafe.[18] Yet they also saw that this form of tenure was the prop of a whole social system and, as such, could not be abolished overnight, along the lines of Free State policy, without doing great harm to the people. Although they sought to contain tribal tenure to the reserves, they also recommended the encouragement of, and provision for a transition to, individual rights to arable plots and residences on the lands set aside for their occupation.[19] Colonel Stanford's dissent, previously noted, pointed out the flaw in this reasoning, which is, perhaps, the major flaw of this Report. This is that localities regarded as unsuitable for Whites offered no attraction to the Black who desired to become a landed proprietor, who usually 'belongs to the civilized class'.[20] The majority of the Commissioners, on the other hand, argued that a free market for land in White areas, with Whites at the same time excluded from purchasing land within Black areas, would favour the subsistence cultivator. 'Their wants are few, and their necessary expenses small. They will buy land at prices above its otherwise market value, as their habits and standard of living enable them to exist on land that it is impossible for Europeans to farm on a small scale.'[21] On the basis of the backward state of agriculture in the reserves ever since, one is bound to conclude that Stanford was correct; and that in accommodating the 'sleeping dog' theory held by White farmers, the Commissioners did not put a firm floor under the Black intelligence and energy that might have directed itself to modern farming. We may surmise that the Commissioners thought this energy would go to the towns.

What then happened, most simply, is that a settled Black labour force in the urban areas did indeed begin to emerge, and politicians became afraid of it. White labour, as I mentioned in the previous chapter, was the first political force to propound the idea of segregated reserves as a way of preventing competition between poor-Whites and Blacks. But the issue for labour was not simply economic but also political and moral. Creswell argued that 'the people who do the actual work of any country eventually inherit that country'.[22] To the economic argument that unskilled White labour was too costly, he contended, from his own experience as a mine manager, that a mine could be worked with a totally White labour force, at White rates of remuneration plus machinery, more efficiently (that is, with lower costs) than with a Black labour force.[23] His opposition to the use of cheap, indentured Black labour as an undercaste, which he regarded as a form of slavery, was that it would bring about a situation in which a White man would not be able to earn a living by the sweat of his brow. Thus he thought that South Africa would deviate at its mortal peril from the model of Australia. Creswell, furthermore, had a puritanical objection to the notion of 'Kaffir work'. He thought that the White man would morally degenerate if he became simply the lowest kind of racial aristocrat, namely, an overseer of cheap Black labour.[24]

Yet labour's *primary* political objective became the institution, not of territorial segregation, but of racial protection in industry. This is not surprising, given the structure of forces within which labour had to weave its way. Not only did it have to contend with the prejudices of White workers themselves. In addition it faced capital's interest and the opinion that 'South Africa is not and can never be a country for the unskilled White labourer'.[25]

It was thus not so much labour by itself as a broader spectrum of political opinion that brought about the change. Afrikaner nationalism, forgetting about Reitz, came to regard itself (and to be regarded) as the 'carrier' of the embryo of the segregation idea from time immemorial. This view could be seen put forth in the National Party's 1947 statement of 'Race Relations Policy'.[26] And there is no question about the historical role that Hertzog played in his agitation for the segregation policy from 1925 and even earlier to 1936. Still, he was joined in his opposition to the extension of the Cape African franchise by such English-speaking figures as Stallard and Heaton Nicholls who were completely articulate in advancing the two notions which, linked together, constituted the essence of the segregation policy. The first was that the Blacks in the towns could not be legally *regarded* as permanently there without giving them the vote on the general franchise. The second was that the denial of this right could be compensated for or rectified by *adding* land to the reserves and making these the centre of Black political life. The agitation from the English-speaking 'anti-assimilationists' is in some respects more interesting than its Afrikaner counterpart because of the fact that the former, by virtue of its political education, had to address itself to the norm of Westminster-style democracy.

In this respect one must recall the comment made by Fagan about the Stallard Commission, 'that it sat at a time when the principle of separate institutions for the different races . . . was still relatively unknown'.[27] What could this mean as applied to an avowed proponent of 'segregation'? Very simply, it meant that the Commission could not entertain the possibility of 'segregation' in a positive respect, which meant among other things in South Africa the right of Blacks to buy land, anywhere in the urban areas. Why not? Here again one sees at work the idea of the 'slippery slope', or a convoluted version of the Westminster norm. This meant that the Whites had to either pretend that the Blacks were all migrants or give them the vote. There was no middle, which Fagan later on, seeing the confusing connotations acquired by the terms 'segregation' or 'separation', began to call 'co-existence'. And the inability to perceive this middle, to repeat emphatically, showed precisely the power of the Westminster norm. If Fagan is correct, one can say that men in the 1920s and 1930s were thinking their way through to what co-existence really meant. But without any precedents, and with a belief that the cities were as 'transitory' as the supply of gold-bearing ore, it is not surprising that in their first attempts at this, they should have fallen back on a conception of territorial segregation or partition between urban and rural areas, which paid lip service to the above norm. Fagan saw, twenty-five years later, that the convolution of this norm was much more injurious to the interests of the permanently settled Black townsmen than a frank recognition of the ethno-political problem. And no one really believed in the fiction that emerged, regardless of how much it enveloped the law.

Dr. Davenport has pointed out, for example, in his thorough analysis of urban Black legislation, that the Natives (Urban Areas) Act of 1923 was a response not so much to abstract ideology as to a concrete need. As such it was in many ways a progressive Act. In response to the epidemics that had broken out in the Black shanty-towns, the Act compelled the municipalities which wanted Black labour to provide hygienic housing arrangements for these workers with, among other things, adequate supplies of pure water. It laid down a framework for the beginnings of local government in the Black townships by the institution of advisory boards. While the Act embodied Stallard's dictum, it in fact left open two courses of action: either the strict implementation of the view that Blacks had no rights in the urban areas, or the partition of the towns into areas where Blacks would also have rights. It did not control the influx of Blacks into the urban areas, which later amendments to the Act sought to do.[28]

Nicholls, with whom Stallard was associated, played a leading role in the 1936 debates on Black representation. He was intransigently opposed to the Black franchise in the Cape and to any representation at all, direct or indirect, for Blacks in the House of Assembly. Against this he stood for the representation of Blacks in the Senate and, eventually, by Blacks themselves. His key conception was a Senate Grand Committee which would have been permanently in session, with Black members to consider Black affairs. He thought the Natives Representative Council, sitting outside Parliament, powerless; and that, presenting resolutions which were then ignored, it could not have avoided becoming a permanent opposition to the Government and a seed-bed of Black nationalism. He was also a leading proponent of the Natives Land Bill of 1936, which sought to add land to the reserves, as promised by earlier legislation. With his eye focused upon the tribesman, there was a certain eccentric quality to his views. He soured on the 1936 legislation, which refused to go along with him on the idea of the Senate Grand Committee. He thought that the compromise creating the three White Native Representatives in the House of Assembly was a cloak behind which the Cape could hide its refusal to allow Blacks to sit in the Senate. He also thought this sacrificed the interest of the 'millions of voteless tribal natives' to the 12,000 detribalized Black voters at the Cape, forgetting that there were many more than 12,000 'detribalized natives' in Johannesburg alone. Eventually he soured even more on the post-1948 regime. By 1959, when he wrote his autobiography, he fully accepted the fact of industrial integration and he said that South Africa would have to face a new Africa in which the old tribal control was weakening.[29] In 1936, however, these were his views in support of the Land Bill:

This Bill has become necessary for these very cogent reasons: First, in order to stem the tide of native immigration to the towns; secondly, *to prevent the emergence of a class struggle in our urban areas*, of which we have had visible signs in the past; thirdly, to create a contented and prosperous native peasantry in our reserves, who will become consumers; fourthly, to prevent the clogging of the industrial advance of the European people who find industrial avenues everywhere filled and crowded with people emerging from the reserves; fifthly, we cannot deal adequately with poor-White problems unless we deal with this congestion of European industry by natives in its initial stages.[30]

Several sentences in this statement bear comment. First of all note the phrase 'prosperous Native peasantry'. In fact there never was (and never will be) a peasantry in South Africa, Black or White. The Black tribesmen and those Whites who became the poor-Whites had a similar economic foundation. They were pastoralists, or to be more precise, 'stock-tenders', with a modicum of cultivation, of a quality that would shame any peasant. One simply has to drive through South Africa today and see the effects of past erosion in both the Black and the White areas to see what this means. The idea that these people, for whom a major source of food-supply was game, were peasants or farmers is simply a myth. In the second place Nicholls spoke of the possibility of an emerging 'class struggle'. He was, of course, referring to the Rand Strike of 1922, of which the upgrading of Black labour had been the triggering cause. Yet when South Africa left the Gold Standard in 1933, it experienced a windfall which generated the rise of new secondary industry. This attracted Black labour which was not displacing but supplementing White labour. Indeed it was not the protectionist legislation acquired by labour but, rather, this industrial expansion that caused the poor-White problem in South Africa to begin to disappear.[31] And this expansion would have been impossible without the Black labour at the base of the industrial economy:

Table 7: Black urban population, 1904–36

Year	Total (in thousands) All races	Blacks	Blacks as % of all races	Index of Blacks (1904 = 100)
1904	1 222	361	29.5	100
1921	1 950	658	33.7	182
1936	3 218	1 252	38.9	347

Source: Statistical Year Book, 1966, table A–22. Percentages and index calculated.

Note: The above census data are adjusted to the 1960 census definition of urban. For other definitions of 'urban', see 'Urbanization 1904–1936', by H. A. Shannon, *South African Journal of Economics*, 5(1937), 164–90.

To this new and irreversible economic fact, and to the needs and problems it created in the towns, the addition of more land to the reserves was fundamentally irrelevant. But then what significance could the land policy have for the well-being of the reserves themselves? For the thinking about this question, which is the practical heart of the segregation policy, one must turn to the *Report of the Native Economic* [Holloway] *Commission 1930–1932*, which went into it in detail and sought to supply a factual foundation for the viability of the policy.

To begin with, this Report was a much more moderate statement of policy than the extremist formulations which had preceded it or came after it in 1948. It fully accepted the existence of *some* permanent Black population in the urban areas and said so in plain words:

A further objection is that the Bloemfontein scheme gives the Natives a fixed interest in the urban area, and therefore encourages their urbanization. Your Commission agrees that it is undesirable to encourage the urbanization of the Native population, but cannot admit that this is a valid objection to the Bloemfontein scheme. It is perfectly clear that a considerable number of Natives have become permanent town dwellers. No good purpose is served by disregarding this fact, or by acting on the assumption that it is not a fact. In the interest of the efficiency of urban industries it is better to have a fixed urban Native population to the extent to which such population is necessary than the present casual drifting population. It is, therefore, better in the national interest to organize the urban areas in such a manner as to give the most satisfactory results. To continue employing Natives in urban areas, but to treat them as if they should not be there, is both illogical and short-sighted.[32]

The Report, as is evident from the above, fully accepted the objective of halting or reducing the drift of Blacks from the reserves to the towns. The majority of the Commissioners, like Nicholls, were haunted by the same spectre of racial conflict and competition for jobs in the urban areas in all their reasoning. Thus they voiced the characteristic consideration that the development of the reserves would offer occupational opportunities for the educated Black, who would otherwise be forced to leave them and then be rebuffed by the social prejudices of White workers. The dissents of Mr. Lucas and Dr. Roberts, which are still instructive today, succinctly pointed out that the Blacks, who were attached to their land, were being pushed off it by the same economic forces operating upon the poor-Whites; that the Blacks emigrating to the towns were the poorest Blacks, who were taking jobs as labourers which Whites did not want; and that the educated Black was precisely the person most likely to find employment among his own people as, for example, a teacher, minister, doctor, clerk, or agricultural demonstrator.[33] We need not comment further about this dimension of the policy.

The originality of the Report, and also its soundness, lay in its assertion that the modernization of the reserves was an absolute necessity for the well-being of the Blacks and of South Africa as a whole. What struck all the Commissioners was the appalling deterioration that had taken place in the reserves since they had been demarcated by the 1913

Land Act. Large parts of them were fast becoming deserts because of overgrazing and man-made erosion.[34] Prior to European conquest these conditions would have been checked by the traditional modes of peaceful or warlike migration. But with the tribes now not only disarmed but confined in their right even to buy land to demarcated reserves, the days of 'easy access to the land' were over. Between the status of scrub cattle in the traditional Bantu culture on the one hand and the effects of modern veterinary medicine on the other, the reserves were overpopulated, not only with people but with grazing animals, beyond their carrying capacity at the prevalent low level of agricultural technique.[35] Yet much of the land, if properly farmed, was good. The reserves in their current condition were an economic liability from every point of view.

The Report recommended the addition of more land to the reserves, not only because it had been promised or because Blacks were demanding it, but in order to relieve the congestion which obstructed the introduction of better methods of land use.[36] But the Commissioners asserted with all due emphasis that more land without better methods would be only a temporary palliative that would see the existing deterioration repeated somewhere else in short order.[37] The Commissioners noted that had an extensive programme of agricultural education taken hold since the Natives Land Act, the situation in the reserves would not have been what it was.[38] Their vision, in short, was the transformation of the Black on the land into a modern agriculturalist and pastoralist by means of an education which penetrated native life. They had high praise for the agricultural colleges for Blacks founded since the Union, but even more so for the work done by agricultural demonstrators, which they thought more important at that time. And they repeatedly asserted the importance of enlisting the help of traditional tribal authority as agents of this educational process.

In recognizing that the traditional norm of 'one man, one lot' would have to give way to the needs of modern agriculture, the Commissioners saw that the latter would have to be reconstituted in the reserves with a smaller number of real farmers.[39] But then having got thus far, the Commissioners lost their way. How would the people who either were landless now or would become surplus to the needs of a more efficient agriculture be economically absorbed? The only answer they could give was small native cottage industry which would not compete with White manufacturing.[40] Altogether they completely lost sight of the role which modern industrialism could play in pulling people not so much 'out of the reserves' but 'off the land' in accordance

with natural economic laws which, together with agricultural education, would lay the foundation of a modernized economy in the
reserves. This blindspot was the effect of being overpowered in
thought by the idea of a segregated or dual economy. Among other
things, this induced the Commissioners to become more mindful on
the one hand of obstacles in custom, and more fearful on the other
hand of deranging traditional Black society than Blacks were themselves. This is shown not only by observations made by such a figure as
Ray Phillips, who was surveying the race problem in South Africa at
about the same time as the Commission and who saw examples of Black
enterprise in agriculture because he was looking for them.[41] It is also
seen in observations cited within the Report itself, especially in the
Addendum by Lucas.[42]

In the late 1940s official policy moved forward with the publication
of two remarkable Reports which addressed themselves to the new
economic realities (and to the loose ends in the *Report of the Native
Economic Commission*). These were the Ninth Report of the Social and
Economic Planning Council, *The Native Reserves and Their Place in
the Economy of the Union of South Africa* (designated herein as the Van
Eck Report), and the Fagan Report, to which I have already referred.
Complementing each other in their economic assumptions and recommendations, both Reports saw the economic problems of the reserves
and the towns as parts of a unified whole. The Van Eck Report put it as
follows:

No reserve policy—not even the policy advocated in this Report—will make
it possible for South Africa to evade the issues raised by the presence of the
Native in European farming areas and in urban areas. These must be considered on their own merits.[43]

Both Reports, furthermore, saw that, like the towns, the reserves
should also be the home of a settled Black population and not simply
a reservoir of migratory and backward labour.[44] The key to progressive
change was a combination of industrialization and modernization of
land use. This would require education, controls to prevent the abuse
of land, changes in land tenure, and accommodations from within the
social structure of the Blacks. But as the Van Eck Report pointed out
there were no magic formulas. While it was true that land conditions
were at their worst where tribal tenure prevailed, individual ownership
had not universally 'turned sand into gold'.[45] The Report itself must
be studied to see what was possible in order to liberate progressive
energy in the reserves in a variety of concrete respects. As to industrialization this would be met in part by rational decentralization which

brought industry to the labour supply. Dr. Van Eck himself was in-
strumental in setting up one of the first decentralization projects, in
King Williamstown, which was economically sound and is still functioning. There would, none the less, be much migration to the existing
urban centres, where the capital to invest in the modernization of the
reserves was being generated, and which needed labour, as is shown by
the following table:

Table 8: Black urban population, 1936–46

Year	Total (in thousands) All races	Blacks	Blacks as % of all races	Index of Blacks (1936 = 100)	(1904 = 100)
1936	3 218	1 252	38·9	100	347
1946	4 482	1 902	42·4	152	527

Source: Statistical Year Book, 1966, table A–22. Percentages and index
calculated.
Note: The above census data are adjusted to the 1960 census definition of urban.

The Fagan Report had a long critique of migratory labour and
followed the Van Eck Report in recommending the aggregation of
Blacks in the reserves into villages. It explicitly took up the question of
how the permanence of the Blacks in the existing cities, which could
neither be altered nor denied, could be dealt with by political arrangements which outflanked the White fears of being politically swamped
and yet did justice to both races. Fagan's standpoint, in the most radical
contrast to a legalistic blueprint, was essentially that of the practical
spirit which addresses itself, first to the facts, and second to what has
to be done. Just as there was a difference between White and Black, so
was there a difference between Black and Black. At issue was thus not
the question of regulation versus laissez-faire, but regulation which concorded with the existing facts. Fagan could then speak about the un-
desirability of compulsion where not necessary as well as of what he
called discrimination for the sake of discrimination.[46]

Apartheid: rhetoric and reality

From the standpoint of these two Reports, the apartheid policy of the
post-1948 Nationalist Government was an attempt to 'turn back the
clock', which both had asserted was impossible. And, indeed, the
increase in the Black population, that had provoked the Fagan Report
in the first place, continued under this very Government (see Tables
9 and 10 over). One cause was the expanded importance in the national
economy of manufacturing relative to mining and agriculture (see
Tables 11 and 12 over).[47]

Table 9: Black urban population, 1946–70

Year	Total (in thousands)		Blacks as % of all races	Index of Blacks	
	All races	Blacks		(1946 = 100)	(1904 = 100)
1946	4 482	1 902	42·4	100	527
1951	5 494	2 391	43·5	126	662
1960	7 474	3 471	46·4	182	961
1970	10 280	4 989	48·5	262	1 382

Source: Statistical Year Book, 1966, table A–22, and Population Census 1970. Percentages and index calculated.

Note: The above census data are adjusted to the 1960 census definition of urban.

Table 10: Trends of White and Black urbanization, 1904–70

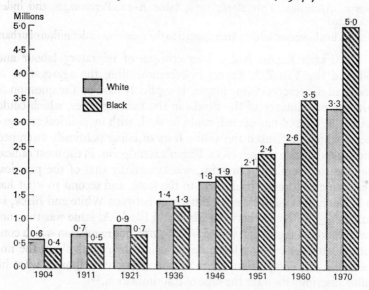

Source: Statistical Year Book, 1966. (*1970 figures are derived from the Population Census, 1970. Bureau of Statistics. Report No. 02–05–01.)

Tables 11 and 12 (opposite): Numbers and wages of Whites and Blacks employed in gold mining compared with the manufacturing and construction industries, for selected years, 1944–75.

Sources: Bulletin of Statistics, various up to 1976; *Statistical News Release,* 13 April 1976; *Chamber of Mines Annual Report,* various up to 1975.

Note: Figures for gold mines exclude those that are not members of the Chamber of Mines.

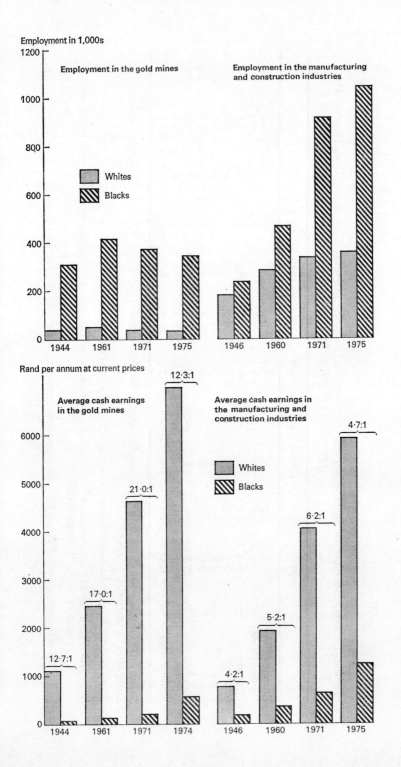

Employment in 1,000s

Employment in the gold mines

Employment in the manufacturing and construction industries

Whites
Blacks

1944 1961 1971 1975

1946 1960 1971 1975

Rand per annum at current prices

Average cash earnings in the gold mines

Average cash earnings in the manufacturing and construction industries

Whites
Blacks

12·7:1 17·0:1 21·0:1 12·3:1

1944 1961 1971 1974

4·2:1 5·2:1 6·2:1 4·7:1

1946 1960 1971 1975

Table 13: A comparison between South Africa and other industrial countries[a] in annual % growth of Gross Domestic Product (by volume) at market prices, 1964–74

	1964	1965	1966	1967	1968	1969	1970	1971	1972	1973	1974
Europe (Six)	5·9	5·0	3·7	3·1	5·9	7·0	5·8	3·6	4·2	5·4	2·4
Europe (Nine)	5·9	4·4	3·3	3·1	5·3	5·8	5·0	3·4	3·9	5·3	2·1
Germany	6·6	5·5	2·8	−0·4	6·7	7·8	6·0	3·1	3·5	4·8	0·4
France	6·3	5·9	4·0	4·8	4·7	7·0	5·9	5·4	5·6	5·6	3·9
U.K.	5·8	2·2	1·9	2·5	3·4	1·1	2·2	2·5	2·6	5·5	0·8
Italy	2·6	3·2	5·8	7·0	6·3	5·7	5·0	1·6	3·1	6·3	3·4
U.S.A.	5·3	6·3	6·6	2·7	4·2	2·6	0·5	3·2	6·1	5·6	−1·9
Japan	13·3	5·1	9·8	12·9	13·5	10·8	10·9	7·3	8·5	10·2	−1·8
South Africa	9·5	9·7	8·5	10·8	7·4	11·3	8·9	10·9	12·2	22·1	19·5[b]

Sources: (Excluding South Africa) 'National Accounts ESA Aggregates 1960–1974'. *Eurostat:* Statistical Office of the European Communities. 1–1975.

South African figures: *Statistical News Release*, p. 12.1, 19 January 1976.

Notes: (a) South Africa's improvement in economic growth rate during 1972 is in strong contrast to most other industrial countries in the Western World.

(b) At constant (1963) prices this still represents a 7·2% increase over the previous year.

Indeed, South Africa from the beginning of the 1960s underwent a boom which would have been impossible, not merely without Black labour, but without a considerable upgrading of settled Black labour. By the mid-'60s White labour in South Africa achieved the condition of virtual full employment (if not over-employment). Thus the supply of labour needed to man the expansion of industry could come only from European immigration, from the local non-Whites or from foreign Blacks from the neighbouring African states. The last are recruited to work in the mines on contracts. The importance and attraction of industry for local Blacks is reflected in the dependence of the mines upon foreign Black labour, which had been increasing over the past decade until external events in 1975 reduced it forcibly.

Table 14: Local and foreign Black mine labour, 1968, 1972, and 1975

	Total	Number employed Local	Foreign	Percentage Local Blacks of Total
1968	382 626	129 947	252 679	34·0
1972	414 333	87 177	327 156	21.0
1975	367 153	125 513	243 640	33·6

Source: Report of the Board of Directors, Mine Labour Organization (Wenela) Ltd., 1969, 1972, and 1975.

As for White immigration from Europe, this had been restricted when the Nationalists came into office on the political grounds that the Afrikaner would be 'ploughed under'. In the 1960s—when the poor-White problem had manifestly disappeared—this restriction was dropped. But immigration could come nowhere near meeting the demand for labour. This was in part due to the fact that in the racial stratification within South African industry non-Whites had a kind of monopoly of the jobs at the base of the industrial system. Thus for a White immigrant to be employable in South Africa he would have to have a skill that was at least superior to that demanded by the jobs which Blacks could and would be permitted to perform.

The upshot of all this is most manifestly seen in the fact that the Government itself became one of the single biggest employers of non-White labour. This was on the Government-owned railways, which in the 1920s had been made a protected sphere for 'sheltered' White labour (*see Table 16 over*).

Table 15: White migration to South Africa, 1948–75

Year	Immigrants	Emigrants	Gain
1948	35 631	7 534	28 097
1951	15 243	15 382	− 139
1954	16 416	11 336	5 080
1956	14 917	12 879	2 038
1957	14 615	10 943	3 672
1958	14 673	8 807	5 866
1959	12 563	9 379	3 184
1960	9 789	12 612	− 2 823
1961	16 309	14 894	1 415
1962	20 916	8 945	11 971
1963	37 960	7 151	30 809
1964	40 865	8 092	32 773
1965	38 326	9 206	29 120
1966	48 048	9 888	38 160
1967	38 937	10 737	28 200
1968	40 548	10 589	29 959
1969	41 466	9 018	32 428
1970	41 523	9 154	32 369
1971	35 845	8 291	27 554
1972	32 776	7 803	24 973
1973	24 016	6 290	17 726
1974	35 847	7 212	28 635
1975	50 349	9 869	40 480

Sources: South African Statistics, various years; *Bulletin of Statistics*, March 1976; *Statistical News Release 29*, March 1976.

Table 16: Employment of Whites and Blacks on South African railways and harbours, for selected years, 1926–75

Year	A: Whites	B: Blacks	A as % of A+B
1926	50 800	44 900	53·1
1933	49 300	28 000	63·8
1938	66 100	54 900	54·6
1948	98 100	89 600	52·3
1950	103 400	84 600	55·0
1968	114 539	93 583	55·0
1970	110 314	96 579	53·3
1972	110 854	99 815	47·4
1975	111 120	116 599	48·8

Sources: Report of the Industrial Legislative Commission of Enquiry, (UG 62–1951), Table 25, 20; *Bulletin of Statistics*, March 1976, Table 2.2.12; *Statistical News Release*.

Thus, while the Minister of Labour was in charge of a policy that sought to keep down the number of Blacks in urban industry, the former Minister of Transport, Mr. Ben Schoeman, was not only hiring non-Whites to do jobs that had formerly been done by Whites but telling objectors, 'You want White railway workers. Find me them.' What is almost comical is that when the Minister of Labour was given the portfolio of Posts and Telegraphs in a cabinet reshuffle, it became apparent that he too was hiring more non-Whites as postmen: which he, indeed, had to do since there were not enough Whites. The Government in business behaved not surprisingly like a business.

But this expansion of non-White labour in the gross is only one part of the story. The other part is that industry in South Africa in the 1960s experienced a kind of social revolution as it became more rationalized. With the introduction of labour-saving machinery the unskilled gang-labour at the base of the old industrial pattern, which did such tasks as 'put and carry work', became more and more superfluous.[48] The flow of materials in factories, for example, which had been traditionally in the hands of this kind of labour, became a big target for such rationalization. Thus the Black labour force of the major employers experienced a transformation from gang-labour to skilled labour or, to be more precise, the kind of semi-skilled labour needed to operate modern machinery. In line with the aims of such organizations as the Productivity and Wage Association, industry instituted training schemes, rational personnel methods, wage scales which reward and stimulate productivity, and pension schemes for its Black labour force. To some degree this has even been stimulated by present Government policy, particularly the Physical Planning and Utilization of Resources Act of 1967, which sought to compel decentralization by putting a ceiling on the number of Black workers in industry (though not in commerce) in the existing industrial centres. This could in principle be an inducement to manufacturers to use their Black labour more efficiently. And there are numerous instances where, after rationalization, the Black wage bill in a given plant increased with a smaller Black work force. Even on the mines, whose requirements for migratory labour are not subject to influx control, the Blacks are put through a short training programme under Black instructors (who are permanently employed). But the process of rationalization has had a much greater scope in secondary industry. This is particularly so in new industry, where vested labour interests have been more flexible than the mining unions, whose whole outlook was formed by the view that the gold mines were a 'perishing asset'.

The above remarks may serve as a general indication of the economic forces with which the Government has had to deal. Now in the face of these forces, in a society which is committed to an expanding standard of living, what has the effect of government policy really been? This policy has had two political cores, which in some respects overlap and in other respects conflict with each other. And we will recognize the same themes that were delineated in the previous section. These are, first, the protection of White labour and second, the fear of being swamped by a common franchise. The restrictions on Blacks entering the towns and the development of the reserves were conceived of as politicized means of alleviating the latter.

As to the former, the story is very simple, and this Government has behaved exactly as did previous governments. The essence of this behaviour is as follows. If an employer wants to upgrade Black labour, and White labour, which has held a veto power since 1924, does not object, because its interests are protected or even advanced, the employer can do what he wants. In small towns in the Northern Transvaal employers in the building industry use Blacks at much higher levels of employment than is possible, at least legally, in Johannesburg. The fact that these employers might be Nationalists is not altogether irrelevant. But the more fundamental fact is this. In these small towns there is no White-labour interest to lodge objections. This reminds one of the old labour pattern in the American South where Blacks were (and still are) able to work at jobs in the building trade, such as masons, from which they were excluded in the North.[49] To say that the South was less 'racist' than the North is a not very precise explanation. We could, of course, by cynical and say that in the South Blacks could work but note vote, whereas in the North they could vote but not work. Underneath all this, of course, as Booker T. Washington clearly saw, was the fact that a White-labour interest, fearful of 'dilution', was not as operative in the South, at least in this sphere, as it was in the North.

To carry this point to the extreme we would have to look at those employments, not in industry but in commerce, where the organized White-labour interest is zero. One such example is market research firms which supply services that have been created by a growing urban Black market. These firms employ Black professionals who, in firms with which I am personally acquainted, earn exactly the same salaries as their White counterparts. Akin to this is the fact that there is now the nucleus of a growing Black managerial class in the field of personnel management. I should also note that some large retailers have opened

'Black' departments, staffed entirely by a Black sales and clerical force. One businessman, who had set up such a department in his business, said to me:

I did not do this for ideological reasons. I am a businessman and this operation has shown a profit.

There are no signs in this firm and there never have been any. When a Black comes in, he is likely to be directed by a White shop assistant to the Black department, which by now he knows about and is looking for. He is, however, completely free to buy anywhere else in the shop, as he did before this department was set up (and where he would have been served by White shop assistants). The Blacks, who have a reputed respect for quality and who, as every businessman in South Africa will tell you, want to buy 'only the best', were understandably suspicious, not so much of separate departments as an abstraction, but rather of the possibility that they were being fobbed off with inferior merchandise. It took them some time before they trusted the set-up. But with its voluntary character and the freedom to compare and see that they are not getting cheated, its reputation was firmly established in the townships. Within the department the top Black shop assistant can earn R10,000 per year. But to do this he has his own private 'organization' working for him in the townships, which sends him customers and to which he pays sub-commissions of about R2–3,000. The department has its own accounts office. When I asked the owner why this was so, he told me that the White bookkeepers couldn't get the Black names right. He also told me that the Black bookkeeper, who handles complicated bookkeeping machinery, was so efficient that he wished he could use her in the general department. Here the social prejudices of the White employees block normal integration. When I was through with the visit to this department, I asked a Black what he thought about it. Did he object to it as 'segregation'?

Well, if I go into a liquor shop and see a wicket marked non-Whites, I will leave that shop to look for another one unless I am desperately short of time. But if I go into a shop and there on one side is an African shop assistant and there on the other is a European, I will go to the African. We talk in our language, we make a little joke, and I don't mind giving him the commission.

These are all examples of Black functionaries serving or connected with a Black clientele, where the White-labour interest, with its characteristic fear of 'dilution' or displacement, is suspended. I could also give examples of Blacks and, more commonly, Coloureds being brought into commercial employment to serve a White or mixed clientele, where the prejudice of White employees is connected not with this economic fear or interest but with the social disinclination against working together with non-Whites as equals in the same unit. But even this varies, depending upon the social prejudices of both the employees and the customers as well as upon the character of the management. One large retail chain, just as it had been the first to bring Afrikaners into the sales force, was the first to bring in Coloureds, whom one can see working side by side with the Whites. Other firms, like the retailer described above, have brought them in as 'teams', making some departments wholly Coloured and others wholly White. But regardless of whether this addition of Coloured staff is done individually or by teams, the fear of dilution or displacement can be dissipated under conditions of expansion where no one—visibly—loses his or her job.

Let us now return from commerce to industry, where the interest of organized White labour is really operative. And one must bear in mind, as noted earlier, that a paramount segment of this Government's electorate in 1948 was and has remained White labour. How does the Government protect this interest or, to be more precise, maintain racial inequality in industry? The key statute is the Industrial Conciliation Act which was an amendment of earlier colour-bar legislation.[50] Under its provisions the Minister of Labour can declare certain jobs reserved for Whites. But this, strange as it may seem, is the most trivial part of the Act and of the whole phenomenon of job reservation or protection. There are only a few jobs which are so reserved, such as lift operators, which are really sheltered employments. As more and more lifts in South Africa are automated, one sees less and less lift operators, White or non-White (who, while not employed as lift operators, also operate lifts). The real heart of the Act that shapes racial inequality is its exclusion of Blacks (but not Coloureds and Indians) from the status of employees under the bargaining provisions of this Act. Whites can form unions which have a legal status under the Act in the settlement of disputes and wage determinations. While Blacks also can form unions, they do not have this legal status; and this Government is implacably opposed to the recognition of Black unions within the provisions of the Act on the political grounds that they would immediately become vehicles for Black nationalism. The Government has not had its ears closed to the need that Black workers have for some means to express their grievances in industry. This was all the more so after the round of strikes in 1973 when, in any number of cases, the management was unable to find a spokesman for the workers or what they wanted. Yet against the Opposition's insistence upon bringing Blacks into the labour movement, the Government's policy is still the expansion and improvement of the works committees established under previous legislation, though they were manifestly ineffective before 1973.

It is this power of the trade unions to co-determine the rate for the jobs to be performed by *both* 'employees' and 'operatives' that is a key source of the racial inequality in industry, or what is called in South Africa the 'wage gap'.* This principle of the 'rate for the job', which seems to be the quintessence of equality, was in fact historically the 'principle' by which non-Whites (and also women) were excluded by organized labour, in South Africa and elsewhere, from industrial employment.[51] The unions can also block access to the kind of on-job training that a worker must have to augment his productivity and skill, which also obviously affects the character of the labour market.[52] This inequality at its polar extreme is that between the skilled White and the totally unskilled migratory tribesman. This was the pattern at the beginning of the industrial revolution, when, as Houghton has noted, there arose a virtual convention that a White man's wage should be five to ten times that of the migratory Black worker.[53] Entering into this judgement was the common view that the migratory Black worker's family, living in the reserves, supported itself on subsistence agriculture and that an increase in Black wages would result in a backward-sloping curve. It was assumed that the native workers, like the Bavarian Catholics in Max Weber's famous analysis, would quit when they had earned what they needed to satisfy their customary wants. In South Africa a common view—which in the 1890s was probably correct—was that the Black came to the gold fields to earn the price of a rifle—three months' work.[54] So long as such conditions prevailed, the White skilled worker hardly needed any 'protection'; and indeed there was no colour bar in the early diamond diggings at Kimberley.

The colour-bar legislation, then and now, operates as a ceiling against settled Black labour; a ceiling, however, which is in tension not only with the demands of this labour but also with the needs of industry for higher numbers of skilled workers, which the shortage of Whites is unable to supply. The kind of inequality between White and Black wages that this makes for in the characteristic industrial hierarchy is very easy to show; and I shall do this in a moment. Before this, however, it may be of some interest in showing the complexity of the South African labour scene, to point out that there is one union which has got around the provisions of the Act. The Clothing Workers

* One should note, however, that these determinations put a floor under the wages of *both*.

Union in the Transvaal set up a sister union for Blacks, which has no legal status as a registered union. The former, however, acts as an agent for the latter and works in complete consultation with it in all representations made under the Act. But this union is virtually in a class by itself. The employees are women; the employers, in the early days of the clothing industry, were Jewish small manufacturers who were sympathetic to the labour movement; and the union has had extraordinarily effective leadership. Furthermore, the labour force in this industry has 'tipped'. First Afrikaner, then Coloured, it is now predominantly Black. Whether this sister-union arrangement will or will not be the model for Black labour in the near future, there are no other examples apart from this one, which is even now seeking recognition as a registered union.

The typical pattern in large-scale industry, including the railways, is that non-Whites are brought into upgraded levels of employment via a reclassification downwards of the job to be performed by the non-Whites. This is a belated effect of the 'civilized' labour policy. In consonance with this policy, jobs which were classified (and remunerated) as skilled in South Africa were jobs which would be classified as semi-skilled in other industrial societies. Management, understandably, has the strongest interest in reclassifying these jobs downward to their true level of skill and to their economic rate; and by and large the upgrading of the non-White in industry takes place via such reclassifications. In new industry in particular, where new technology is used, reclassification of a job (from artisan to operative) typically goes hand in hand with the splitting up of old jobs into new ones, though this is not universally the case. In any event this process requires the consent of White labour. The latter can always try to make a stand on the principle of the rate for the job, to block the racial changeover. For example, the Building Workers Union in 1972 came out with a statement that most non-South Africans would find unintelligible. This was: 'since job reservation has failed to protect the White man, we must now return to the principle of the rate for the job'. But since industry would have to close down operations without upgrading Black labour (a fact of which White labour is fully aware), this is just rhetoric. What White labour has in fact been doing, in industries where it is still numerous enough to make a stand, is to make a kind of 'deal' with management. It agrees to the advancement of non-Whites into superior positions, demanding for itself rises as its part of the bargain, thus making sure of a bigger 'share of the pie'.

This process of upgrading non-White labour in industry is characteristically 'managed' in sociologically evident ways to accommodate the prejudices and fears of the White workers. Where non-Whites are brought in to do the same job that Whites still perform, the job, to begin with, is given a different title and there is spatial segregation of the labour force into racial teams. On the railways, for example, there are White 'shunters' and Black 'marshallers' doing exactly the same job in different railway yards, at a wage differential (to use the 1972 figure) of about 2 to 1.* If the Whites had stood firmly on the principle of the rate for the job, the Blacks would not be working at all. In one large factory through which I was being shown by the White personnel manager, I was taken through bay after bay where the labour force had been totally 'Africanized'. Finally, we got to a large room, in the middle of which was a four-foot brick wall with two swinging gates. On one side of the wall were White die-makers. On the other side were, in this case, not Black but Coloured die-makers, who had just been brought into employment. They were doing exactly the same work, although the Whites were classified and were being paid as artisans, the Coloureds as operatives, with a wage differential of about $2\frac{1}{2}$ to 1. The manager said to me that the Coloureds were better workers than the Whites. I eventually asked the manager about the curious wall in the middle of the room which I could see was a makeshift. He told me that without that wall the union would never have agreed to the entry of the Coloureds, for whom this work was an advancement in both salary and level of work performed. In yet another factory through which I was taken by a Black personnel manager, I once again saw bay after bay of Black workers using machines. As we were returning to the office, I noticed an old White man working out in the open behind a building. He was operating a machine with a 'Native boy' who was handing him steel rods and taking them away after they had been bent by the machine. Not being technically minded, I did not really notice what he was doing. The Black official then called my attention to the fact that he was doing exactly the same operation as the Blacks in the first bay were doing by themselves, without 'Native boy' assistants. But he was near retirement and incapable of being upgraded himself. So he was being kept on but concealed behind a building, where he did his work in the old traditional pattern. In the firm previously mentioned, the manager told me that when the racial change-over took place, a White who was being displaced was offered a supervisory position in another part of the factory. But to do this he would have had to learn the details of the

* By 1976 this differential had narrowed to about $1\frac{1}{2}$ to 1.

4

new job to be supervised under the direction of a Black straw-boss, which he refused to do. So he quit.

This whole process by which Blacks in particular are brought into industry is really a process in which the White unions themselves acquiesce in a form of 'rate-busting'. It is curious to recall that the rationale of the labour movement in South Africa as elsewhere was to prevent precisely this. Yet the unions are now prepared to go along with it. The shortage of White labour is such that they really have no choice, and in the main they have nothing to lose. To be sure some Whites, incapable of being pushed up, will be pushed out. In fact, if South Africa had more extensive welfare provisions, 'sheltered employment' for Whites, which is a form of welfare, would have disappeared altogether.

All this makes for the conclusion that there are not one but rather two aspects to the 'wage gap'. The first is the one between the efficient White, who is upgraded by the reclassification process, and the Blacks, who are less efficient or productive at the moment when they are brought into the labour force. The productivity factor is obviously connected with the fact that Blacks do not have compulsory schooling. In one plant which I visited, which had recently changed its entire labour force of two hundred from White to Black with one exception, the White foreman, who was from England, put it to me as follows:

Personally I have no trouble with these Africans, and they are a good lot. But my job would be much easier if the working force were White. The White can read, he can handle figures, he is quicker. He has a Standard VII education. But the management did not see it that way.

When I asked him whether a Black with a Standard VII education would not also be quicker, he said:

Do you think an African with a Standard VII would work in the plant? He would want to be a clerk or nothing.

This plant was interesting in that every Black in it was illegally performing certain operations which only the White was supposed to do, a practice which has long been widespread in the country. When I asked the foreman what would happen if a government inspector walked in, he said, 'Well, that is what the White is there for.' Thus it would appear that the White and the Blacks on the bench were really doing the same work but at very unequal rates of pay. But then the foreman pointed out to me huge piles of defective work which had been done improperly by the Blacks and which had to be corrected by the White man, who served among other things as a kind of trouble-shooter.

Table 17: Black and White wages in factory 'A', 1960–70
(averaged for all workshops)

I. Wage differentials (in cents per hour)

	Black (Labourer)	Black (Semi-skilled)[a]	White (Semi-skilled)[a]	White (Artisan)
1960 Statutory min.[b]	11·72	16·05	49·90	66·94
Aver. employee	15·30	17·20	50·00	77·50
1963 Statutory min.	16·00	20·00	73·77	76·33
Aver. employee	17·50	20·00	77·00	94·00
1965 Statutory min.	17·00	21·50	81·50	86·50
Aver. employee	18·50	21·50	84·00	114·00
1968 Statutory min.	19·00	22·00	84.00	91·00
Aver. employee	21·00	24·00	91·00	146·00
1970 Statutory min.	21·00	25.00	100·00	105·00
Aver. employee	23·00	25·00	104·00	150·00

% increase, 1960–70:				
Statutory min.	79·2	55·8	100·4	56·9
Average	50·3	45·3	108·0	93·5

II. Wage differentials expressed in ratios

Intra-racial	1960	1970
Black semi-skilled to Black labourer		
Statutory min.	1·4:1	1·2:1
Average	1·12:1	1·09:1
White artisan to White semi-skilled		
Statutory min.	1·3:1	1·1:1
Average	1·6:1	1·4:1
Inter-racial		
White semi-skilled to Black labourer		
Statutory min.	4·3:1	4·8:1
Average	3·3:1	4·5:1
White semi-skilled to Black semi-skilled		
Statutory min.	3·1:1	4·0:1
Average	2·9:1	4·2:1
White artisan to Black labourer		
Statutory min.	5·7:1	5·0:1
Average	5·1:1	6·5:1
White artisan to Black semi-skilled		
Statutory min.	4·17:1	4·2:1
Average	4·5:1	6·0:1

Notes: (a) There are different grades of semi-skilled work, so that care must
be exercised if comparing the averages above with the average wage
rates for selected job categories given in Table 18.
(b) The statutory rates have been adjusted to include the minimum
cost of living allowance.

In a large plant with a sizeable White labour force, the typical racial pattern of wages was as set out in Table 17. I say 'was' deliberately because these figures carry the story only up until 1970, and there has been considerable pressure to raise wages and the productivity of Black labour since 1973. None the less, these figures give one an indication about the background of the agitation which continues over the issue of the wage-gap. These figures are the salary schedule of one firm over a period of years. This is a sociologically interesting firm as it has not only 'Africanized' its labour force to a great extent, but uses the most advanced machinery.

Table 18: Black and White wages in factory 'A', 1960–7

(Average hourly rates paid for normal time in three workshops)

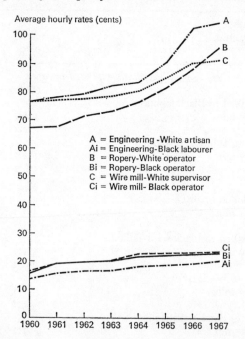

Not to be confounded by statistics, I would suggest that the reader look at Table 18. This shows in graphic form the gap between White and Black industrial wages. One can see how the inter-racial gaps increased during this period, especially with regard to average wages, while the intra-racial gaps decreased. Of all the categories of labour the semi-skilled White made the biggest percentage gains and the semi-skilled Black the least. The latter was not holding his own, relative to other categories, White and Black. Note the relative position of Black operators (Ci) and Black labourers (Ai), which is based on the wages in three of the shops in the factory under discussion.

As noted earlier the wage gap has two aspects, the first of which is that between the skilled White at the top and the unskilled Black at the bottom. This differential between skilled and unskilled earnings, which in South Africa is correlated with race, is higher in South Africa than in ethnically homogeneous countries and particularly those with a welfare state policy. Thus if one compares South Africa at one extreme

Table 19: Estimated unskilled earnings in selected Western European countries, the United States, and South Africa, as a percentage of skilled earnings

Denmark (1965):	81%
France (1964):	69%
West Germany (1965):	80%
Italy (1959):	81%
Norway (1964):[a]	87%
United Kingdom (1960):	67%
United States of America (1958):[b]	64%
South Africa (c. 1961):[c]	20%

Sources: UN Economic Survey of Europe in 1965: Part 2, 'Incomes in post-War Europe: a study of policies, growth and distribution', Chapter 5, pp. 28–9, table 5.16, Geneva 1967. Figure for South Africa is from *The South African Economy* by D. Hobart Houghton, 4th edn., 1967, p. 162. Percentages calculated. N.B. International comparisons are extremely difficult to make and are shown only as a rough guide.

Notes: (a) Refers to mechanical engineering industry only.
(b) Semi-skilled and skilled workers grouped together.
(c) Refers to private manufacturing and construction industries only.

with Norway at the other, unskilled earnings as a percentage of skilled earnings are 20% and 87% respectively. For the United States the figure is 64%. But in South Africa Black and White wages have by no means been simply a constant function of each other. Before the War Black wages were advancing relative to White wages.[55] In the recent period the gap has widened. Today the agitation about the wage gap is aimed at giving the Black workers a bigger 'slice of the pie', since across-the-board percentage increases for all races obviously widen the gap. After the round of strikes in 1973 there were indeed widespread

Table 20: Wage comparisons by race and year in a builder's and decorator's firm in Johannesburg, 1965, 1973, and 1975[a]

	(Average Weekly Earnings in Rand)				
	Whites		Blacks		
	Highest paid job	Lowest paid job	Semi-skilled		Unskilled
			Highest[c]	Lowest[d]	Labourer[e]
	A	B	C	D	E
1965	50·64	43·43	17·00	12·96	11·80
1973	100·00	70·96	38·00	22·12	19·56
1975 Basic	96·00	88·00	60·00	42·80	21·20
Overtime	28·80	26·40	18·00	12·80	6·32
Total[b]	124·80	114·40	78·00	55·60	27·52

The intra-race wage gap

	A as ratio of B	C as ratio of E
1965	1·17:1	1·44:1
1973	1·40:1	1·94:1
1975	1·69:1	2·83:1

The inter-race wage gap

	A as ratio of C	B as ratio of C	A as ratio of E
1965	2·98:1	2·55:1	4·29:1
1973	2·63:1	1·87:1	5·11:1
1975	1·60:1	1·47:1	4·53:1

Notes: (a) These figures may be taken as typical of firms in the building industry, although earnings tend to be higher in Johannesburg than elsewhere in the country. For this firm the week is 40 hrs.
(b) The totals for each year exclude the value of industrial stamps and other benefits, some of which may be cashed-in.
(c) Operator Grade 1.
(d) Learner Operator Grade 2.
(e) Lowest paid.

increases for Blacks; and foreign companies, particularly British companies, became subject to the pressure of British public opinion to pay higher wages to their Black employees. To all this the Government, while standing firm in its opposition to the formation of registered Black unions that would be brought under the Industrial Conciliation Act, replied that there is no maximum to what a White employer can pay a Black, which is legally correct.

But then there is the second aspect of the wage gap. This is the manifestation of the colour bar or of racial discrimination, pure and simple, which takes the form either of paying racially unequal wages to the equally skilled, or of excluding Blacks from the training for superior positions. The first form is to be seen, characteristically, outside industry in the statutory differentials for the public employees of the state or of the municipalities, such as teachers, doctors and nurses, bus-drivers. As was the case in the old American South these differentials are a reflection of the political inequality of the various racial groups in the society as a whole. An indication of how much the atmosphere in South Africa has changed in this respect, however, is the effectiveness of agitation both by non-Whites and, more decisively, by Whites to eliminate these differentials. The White doctors who work in provincial non-White hospitals have been particularly vocal; and the direction in which all this points is now manifestly clear.

In industry too differentials of precisely this type exist. I noted earlier the example of Coloured die-makers whose work was of a not inferior quality to that of their White counterparts. And in general it is the case that no matter how unskilled a person is when he enters the labour force, he can acquire, by no more than intelligently watching, experience that increases his skill. In fact the whole fear of dilution among the White gold-miners rested not on the hypothetical assumption that this might happen. It rested rather on the fact that, from the beginning of industrialized mining, the Whites themselves had been turning over to the Blacks the superintended operations which the Blacks were not legally supposed to do.

The most glaring causes, however, not simply of inequality but of a discontinuity between White and Black wages in the industrial structure have been the impediments to training Blacks for advanced positions. But it was precisely here that Government policy underwent a decisive change. The Prime Minister, in an address to the annual conference of the Motor Industries Federation in October 1973, stated:

It should be clear that in terms of Government policy there is nothing to prevent employers, with the co-operation of the trade unions, taking the necessary steps to bring about improvements in the productive use of non-White labour.[56]

He added that 'it would be of little use if new, more advanced jobs were opened up to Blacks if they were unable to take advantage of them because of lack of training'. The Prime Minister then continued:

Not so long ago few South Africans holding the type of office which I occupy would have the courage to say what I am about to say. That is that no White South African should be entitled to rely on the colour of his skin to ensure for him a particular job or occupation.[57]

We may readily grant that no prime minister, and certainly no Nationalist prime minister could have spoken this way until the poor-Whites had disappeared as a political class. And relevant, too, to this new posture is the growing number of non-Afrikaners—Greeks, Portuguese, Italians—in the White industrial labour force.

But equally sensitive, perhaps even more so, is this question of skilled training, or, as the Prime Minister delicately put it, 'improvements in the productive use of non-White labour'. Industry, to be sure, had been providing training for years at the highest level which the unions would permit. But for a prime minister publicly to acknowledge not only its right of existence but also its desirability at advanced levels, strained against the second pole of Nationalist policy, namely, the fear of the consequences of political integration on a one-man, one-vote basis. As mentioned earlier, this took the form of reaffirming as an article of faith Stallard's definition of all Blacks in the towns as transients or 'temporary sojourners', against the recommendations of the Fagan Report. When faced with the obvious *de facto* permanence of the settled Black population in the towns, Nationalist rhetoric even came up with the formulation that 'some' Blacks in the towns were 'temporarily permanent'! The very word 'permanence' had become a redherring in South African politics. Now training obviously implies permanence. Permanence raises the age-old question about the political rights of the Blacks in the cities. This is the political concern, over and above the protection of White labour, which has enveloped the whole of South African politics.

As we have seen, the labour policy, however baldly it asserted the primacy of the interests of the White worker, was none the less clear and distinct enough to permit practical modifications. By contrast the political objectives of the regime were and still remain much more ambiguous with respect to both ends and means. These objectives became the basis of the most grandiose schemes of both political and economic reconstruction, and of the most doctrinaire politics.

Dr. Verwoerd, as Minister of Bantu Affairs and then as Prime Minister (1958–66), evolved what is often called the 'grand design' of political apartheid. As projected by him this structure was first and foremost a rhetorical 'No' to the idea of representation by way of a common franchise, but it was one which at the same time was full of practical problems and objections. The Coloureds and the Indians were each

Table 21: Population census of 1970 compared with that of 1960

(Population in thousands)

Republic

	1960	%	*1970*	%	*1960–70* % *change*
Whites	3 088	19·3	3 779	17·7	+22·4
Coloureds	1 509	9·4	1 996	9·4	+32·3
Asians	477	3·0	614	2·9	+28·7
Blacks	10 928	68·3	14.893	70·0	+36·3
Total	16 002	100·0	21 282	100·0	

White Areas

Whites	3 064	25·8	3 761	26·2	+22·8
Coloureds	1 494	12·6	1 983	13·8	+32·7
Asians	471	4·0	611	4·3	+29·7
Blacks	6 827	57·6	7 975	55·7	+16·8[a]
Total	11 856	100·0	14 330	100·0	

Black Homelands

Whites	24	0·6	18	0·3	−25·0
Coloureds	15	0·4	13	0·2	−13·3
Asians	6	—	3	—	−50·0
Blacks	4 101	99·0	6 918	99·5	+68·7[a]
Total	4 146	100·0	6 952	100·0	

Sources: Department of Statistics, *Population Census*, 6 Sept. 1960, Vol. 7, No. 1, and *Hansard*, Vol. 10, cols. 5132–3, 25 Sept. 1970. Percentages calculated.

Note: In considering these percentages the following should be noted: that the 1960 census is generally considered to have been under-enumerated; that a large number of urban Blacks probably avoided being included in the census; and that in some cases, due to boundary adjustments, Blacks included in the White areas in 1960 are now included in the 1970 census in Black reserves, although no movement of Blacks may have occurred. (On these points, see *Survey of Race Relations 1970*, pp. 134–5.)

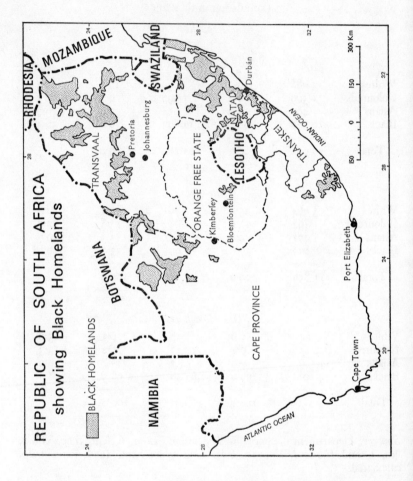

REPUBLIC OF SOUTH AFRICA
showing Black Homelands

BLACK HOMELANDS

RHODESIA

MOZAMBIQUE

SWAZILAND

TRANSVAAL

Pretoria

Johannesburg

ORANGE FREE STATE

Kimberley

Bloemfontein

LESOTHO

NATAL

Durban

TRANSKEI

INDIAN OCEAN

Port Elizabeth

BOTSWANA

CAPE PROVINCE

Cape Town

NAMIBIA

ATLANTIC OCEAN

300 Km
150
0
150

24

28

32

32

28

24

20

24

28

32

to have their own representative councils to administer their own affairs, which people began to talk of as parliaments. At once the objection arose of what power they had or could have compared with the 'real' parliament which passed the laws and controlled the purse-strings. What could they be except the organs of subordinate 'nations within a nation'? Anticipating these very objections, the Government at the outset appointed sufficient members to get a majority on the Coloured Representative Council who would accept the separate framework. The results were exactly what one might expect. Two 'parties' immediately emerged, essentially the appointed and elected members of the Council, the deliberations were in large part a series of resolutions protesting against apartheid, and the institution visibly began to flounder. At that point the present Prime Minister appointed the (Theron) Commission of Inquiry into Matters Related to the Coloured Population Group, consisting for the first time of both Whites and Coloureds. With regard to the Blacks, Dr. Verwoerd, as we noted in Chapter I, pressed forward with the one element in the apartheid idea that even remotely approximated to the idea of territorial separation or partition. It was he who first stated that the Blacks could have political independence, if they wanted it and when they were prepared for it, within the boundaries of the old Native reserves laid down by the 1936 legislation. With augmentation and consolidation of land, this would make for nine 'homelands' corresponding to the main ethnic divisions among the Blacks.

At once the age-old objection arose of what was to be the status of almost two-thirds of the Black population living outside the home-lands? Cognizant of this objection, which had been voiced at the time of the 1936 legislation, the Department of Bantu Affairs, which was beginning to act like a government within the Government, appointed, as in the case of the Coloureds, sufficient members (chiefs and head-men) of the Black territorial legislatures to get a majority in favour of its policy. Moreover the Government, in implementing this framework, made an assault on anything it saw as a 'precedent for integration' that was more doctrinaire and harsh than was anything under Malan. This concerned such things as trading rights and the right of home-owner-ship in the townships. But then, in addition, Dr. Verwoerd blocked the key recommendations of the Tomlinson Report about capital invest-ment in the reserves. This too was seen as a 'precedent for integration'. As a result the developmental aspect of the policy became so politicized that it was stifled.

About 1970 the inevitable happened. The Black leaders who had come to power under this framework began to voice the obvious complaints about the doctrinaire restrictions imposed by Dr. Verwoerd's policy. Chief Buthelezi, the Chief Councillor of Kwa-Zulu, presented a particularly articulate inaugural address in which he characterized apartheid as an arrangement by which the White man got the fat and the Black man got the bone. In short order South Africa began to discover the significance of what was seen as the key factor in the Soweto riots of 1976, namely, the absence of effective consultation between the Government and the permanently settled Black townsmen. And it was precisely this right of normal consultation, along the lines recommended by the Fagan Commission, which the doctrinaires in the Government thought had been rendered superfluous by the actualization of the homeland administrations.

As a clue to the dynamics in the situation, as it concerns all the non-White groups, we must look at the relations between the Government and the Coloureds. The political change that could take place in their situation, if reason prevails, may prove to be a kind of practical key to the race problem in its entirety.

As mentioned earlier, the Coloured Representative Council in its original form was not working. Why? As an official of the Council put it to me, the Coloureds did not trust the Government. They had already been embittered by the experience of being taken off the common electoral roll in the Cape. And the use by the Government of its powers to appoint members to get a seemingly pro-apartheid majority discredited the C.R.C. altogether. Then in 1974 the anti-Government Coloured Labour Party, in the second election to the C.R.C., once again won a majority of the elected seats. This time the Government prudently announced that it would appoint the head of the Coloured Labour Party as chairman of the council executive. But a confrontation situation developed at once. This party, standing for the restoration of the Coloureds to the common roll, had declared that it would boycott the C.R.C. if it won the election. And, indeed, within six days of convening the first session of the new council, the Labour Party executive adjourned the C.R.C. for six months, announcing that the Government would have to indicate exactly what it envisaged for the Coloured people before they would reconvene. The Government then dismissed the executive and appointed a Coloured Administrator (to discharge the statutory functions of the executive). In the aftermath the Theron Commission reported, at the very end of the parliamentary session, in June 1976.

The Labour Party, which had boycotted the sittings of the Commission, welcomed the recommendations of the Report. This was not surprising. The spirit of the Theron Report is essentially a restoration of the practical spirit of the Fagan Report. Thus its mere appearance is perhaps the most amazing thing that has happened in South Africa since this Government came to power. When the Commission was first appointed, it was generally expected that whatever recommendations it made would be projected wholly within the framework of orthodox apartheid. In fact the majority recommendations mentioned neither this term nor its opposites because they did not reason in terms of the 'integration–segregation' polarity. With a major emphasis upon a judicious combination of uplift and self-help, the recommendations sought altogether to humanize an orientation which accepted the existence of separate social communities, as a fact or necessity rather than as a virtue, in a society within which all rise or fall together. The comprehensive object which the Commission enjoined upon South Africa for the Coloured people was thus nothing less than the elimination of the status of the Coloureds as a politically alienated, hostile, impoverished, powerless undercaste. And it saw the means of actualizing this goal in ways which transcended the crude and harsh polarity of either 'develop yourselves' by going out of sight, or 'let us develop you', as if human beings were the matter of a Stalinist technicism.

In the present context we concern ourselves with the constitutional question of political rights which the Commission raised in its concluding recommendation.[58] This contains two main points. The first is the necessity for a direct voice in the Government, at all levels, for the Coloureds. The second is the necessity to adapt the conventional Westminster norms in the process of constitutional adjustment:

Since the Coloured population has no direct share or say in the decisive legislative institutions of the Republic of South Africa (i.e. Parliament, provincial councils, municipal councils and rural local authorities), and the successful development of the alternative measures taken for purposes of Coloured representation and self-determination is being hampered by strong opposition from the vast and effective majority of Coloureds, as well as by constitutional anomalies which in the opinion of the Commission cannot be eliminated satisfactorily and adequately, the Commission recommends that:
(a) *with a view to the further extension of the political civil rights of Coloureds and the creation of opportunities for more constructive participation and co-operation, provision be made for satisfactory forms of direct Coloured representation and a direct say for Coloureds at the various levels of government and on the various decision-making bodies;*
(b) *with a view to the implementation of the proposal above, a committee of experts be appointed to make more detailed proposals in regard to the organizational and statutory adjustments required, provided that due regard shall be*

*had to all the problems and considerations set forth fully in Chapters 17 to 21 of
this report;*
(c) *in the process of constitutional adjustment it will have to be accepted that the
existing Westminster-founded system of government will have to be changed to
adapt it to the specific requirements of the South African plural population
structure.*[59]

What should be pointed out in these recommendations with all due
emphasis is their practical character. It can be summarized into these
two questions: what is put forth as the general rule and what, correla-
tively, as the exception to the rule. The answers to these are what im-
parts to this as to any practical proposal its political intention and
spirit. They are in fact the decisive element in a political proposal. We
can see all this somewhat more clearly by comparing the majority
recommendation with that of the minority, who objected to the para-
graphs cited above (as well as a number of others). It is of interest that
the minority recommendation began with paragraph (c) above, which
it restated almost word for word. But to begin in this way is to seek to
make the exception the rule. We may find significant the one word
which the minority recommendation added in its opening sentence:

(a) in the process of constitutional *development* and adjustment . . .*

When the Theron Report was tabled in Parliament, it was praised
by both the English and the Afrikaner press. The Government itself
at once announced its rejection of recommendation 178. Afrikaner
commentators, however, pointed out that the Government, which
accepted most of the recommendations, did not indicate precisely
which ones they accepted. The intention behind this commentary,
which was not quite true, is obvious; and it would be judicious to
recognize that at this writing the Theron Report, which is not yet
available in English, has not had time to permeate public opinion. We
should also note that all but one of the White members of the majority
on the Commission were Nationalists. The Prime Minister has for
some time held out the idea of an inter-Cabinet council with representatives of the Coloureds and the Indians. The Indians voted to accept
this, and the Prime Minister will shortly hold discussions with Coloured
leaders about establishing such a council with them also. If these
councils succeed in getting the confidence of the Indian and Coloured
leaders, to do which the latter must be able to 'deliver the goods', they

---

* For the South Africanologist the word 'development' in this context means no
direct say in the government.

will work. By working from the top down, they may prove to be the most practical way to establish trust between the Government and the non-White population groups.

Let us now turn from the political to the more strictly economic aspect of government policy. The Government held forth the goal of separate (that is, economic) development for all three of the non-White groups and, indeed, established development corporations to lend money for entrepreneurship by all three on a seemingly parallel plane. Underneath all this was at work the notion of Coloured, Indian, and Black 'economies'. This in part flowed from Afrikaner nationalism's self-understanding of its history. The Afrikaners, under nationalist inspiration, had developed a whole range of commercial institutions. The others, for their own good, should do so as well. But all this overlooked two decisive facts. The first is that the Afrikaner achievement in commerce, however impressive, did not constitute an 'Afrikaner economy'. The second is that it did not have to surmount legal obstacles. The Theron Report prudently rejected the notion of a 'Coloured economy'.

It was only with regard to the Blacks that the idea of separate development culminated in a massive utopian project for socio-economic reconstruction. Thus we may confine our discussion to their experience for the light it sheds about the general problem of this chapter, namely, the relation between economics and politics.

The crux of the matter is that the project was unambiguously politicized. The reserves were to be developed not, for example, to alleviate the Black poverty therein, but rather to reduce the number of Blacks in the towns. And the gist of the following remarks can be summarized in two sentences. The first is that the politicization of the project impeded the modernization of the reserves. The second is that, far from 'solving', it in fact aggravated the problem of the Blacks in the towns. We deal with these points in turn.

As noted earlier, Dr. Malan, in response to the prodding of the Opposition about when total separation was to be achieved, appointed the (Tomlinson) Commission for the Socio-Economic Development of the Bantu Areas within the Union of South Africa, which published an abridged version of its Report in 1955.

The Commission saw that there was neither enough Black capital nor entrepreneurship to get industries started in the reserves. It, therefore, recommended that both Whites and the Government would have to act as entrepreneurs for 'a considerable time'. It stipulated, however, the following three conditions:

(1) Bantu must be employed as far as possible; in those occupations in which Bantu cannot be engaged within a short time, provision must be made for training (in co-operation with the authorities where necessary), so that these posts can also be filled by Bantu as soon as possible;

(2) Bantu investors and the Development Corporation must have the first option of taking over the share interests of European entrepreneurs who wish to withdraw; and

(3) European entrepreneurs must aim at allowing the Bantu to participate progressively in the management of, as well as in investment in, undertakings.[60]

This recommendation, which was the subject of a minority dissent by two members of the Commission, was then vetoed by Dr. Verwoerd, to the dismay of the *verligtes* in the National Party. A number of them broke with him on this question. To their continual objections that without White investment very little would take place in the reserves, his invariable reply was that it would become a precedent for integration or that 'one must not force the pace'. The net effect of this erratic policy, however, was to hamstring the economic inclinations of both Whites *and* Blacks towards the development of the reserves.

To begin with, Dr. Verwoerd sought to solve the conflict between integration and the needs of development by restricting but also directing White capital to the borders of the reserves. The Physical Planning Act, as noted, put a ceiling on Black employment in manufacturing (but not commerce) in the existing urban areas. Under the border industries scheme capital could be brought to the reserves in apparent consistency with the tenets of the apartheid policy. Factories would be located right on the borders of Black homelands. The workers would live in new townships inside these homelands where there would be no obstacles to their owning houses freehold. Thus integration, in the sense understood by this policy, would not arise. There would also be greater opportunities for employment at higher levels than in the towns. The encouragement of decentralization to these border areas had in fact been recommended by the Tomlinson Commission; and though this scheme was rhetorically hailed by the Government in the 1960s as a 'solution', it was not *ipso facto* economically retrograde. The reason is that the largest border complexes are in the metropolitan areas of Pretoria, Durban, and East London. I interviewed a plant manager of a company in Rosslyn, the 'border' area near Pretoria, which had recently relocated there from East London. I asked him whether the Government had given the company any inducement to relocate. He said 'yes', and then, to my surprise, added:

But we would have moved here anyway.
Really?
Of course. We are now in the heart of the biggest market in South Africa.

As for Black entrepreneurs, the kernel of government policy for many years was the presupposition that they would only participate in these rural projects if they were pressured to relocate from the towns. Thus in the first place the Government imposed restrictions on the scope of Black business activity in the urban townships. As noted earlier, Blacks were given a racial monopoly of trading sites in these townships, which has stimulated the expansion of a Black middle class. But there is a ceiling placed on what they can sell—namely, necessaries—and on the number of businesses they can own. Furthermore, they cannot own the land (because the Black township was defined as a White area). Hence, they are unable to use land as collateral in getting loans from commercial banks. They also cannot form partnerships and companies that transcend the homelands. If these Black traders, many of whom are former teachers, had more commercial experience than they possess, they would still find it difficult with their undercapitalized businesses to compete with Indian and White businesses located outside the residential townships.

The obverse side of this restriction in the towns is that the Government did set up investment corporations for the various ethnic groups to lend money to qualified entrepreneurs for starting or expanding businesses. Among the Blacks it imposed the condition at the very beginning that they relocate from the towns to the homelands. Where this concorded with economic realities, it made sense and was seen as such by the people concerned. The leading Black industrialist in South Africa, who manufactures furniture, and who began in the Black township of Johannesburg, accepted a loan under these conditions, relocating to Hamanskraal in the Bophutatswana homeland. And in fact, as he told me, not only are his labour costs lower there but his labour is better, which is the way any businessman would talk. He has since not only expanded his business but completely rationalized the production process. Later on the Bantu Investment Corporation dropped the iron-clad requirement of compulsory relocation. But, as the director of the corporation told me, many of the Black businessmen, finding their businesses in the homelands more profitable than those in the towns and being unable to manage both, voluntarily 'relocated' or decentralized their business. Under this policy there has been a visible movement of Blacks into mainly service businesses in the homelands—general stores, petrol stations, transportation (taxis and buses), even a few hotels. Some of this is very impressive. Some of it is (or was) absurd. Eight years ago, I interviewed one small trader in the North financed by the Bantu Investment Corporation whose whole stock could fit into a good-sized cupboard. He told me that if he could, he would move to Pietersburg to get a job. But this marginal (or, really, sheltered) enterprise would disappear if the development project were 'depoliticized'.

More significantly the Government failed to see that many of the businessmen in the towns should have been encouraged to stay right where they were, to expand, and then to branch out into the homelands with their own capital, following natural economic laws. In this way such economic activity in the homelands would represent a real net increment to their economies, and not simply a transfer of activity from White hands to Black. The urban economy, instead of being seen as something opposed to the rural economy, would thus become a bridge to the development of the latter. One project mooted to me by Black businessmen is that of a market in Soweto for edibles produced by Black cultivators in the homelands, who under the stimulus and direction of the Black traders in the town, would be brought more intensely into the modern economy. One such businessman spoke to me as follows:

As you know everything today is organization. The European is organized in chain stores and companies and we have to do the same thing in order to survive. What we businessmen in Soweto want to do is to organize a market for food, using our own sources of supply in the country.

I then asked him:

Could you really compete with the chain stores in town?

Yes. As you know our costs of living are lower. And provided we organized the whole thing from beginning to end, including the transport, we could meet the competition of the chain stores.

As this Black summed it up to me, 'What we want is a green light in both town and country.'

At the present time, it is estimated that the homelands, which contain somewhat more than a third of the whole Black population of South Africa and a fourth of the whole population of the country, contribute less than 1% to the national economy of South Africa. They are still undeveloped, populated overwhelmingly by women, children, and old men who live on remittances earned in the towns. One should not, however, underestimate what the Government has done in the way of planning and creating an infrastructure for the development of these areas. It has not stood still. Nor have the Blacks themselves who, far from giving up and succumbing in the face of doctrinaire restrictions, grabbed hold of what opportunities presented themselves and plunged forward despite these rigidities. I will give one example. I know a Black agronomist, trained in the United States, who ten years ago set up a nursery for shrubs and seedlings in Johannesburg. This would have been illegal in the Black township where Black business was then limited to food, dry-cleaning, and service stations. He did it, however, on rented land in the White area on the border of the township. When the Government found out about this they put a stop to it. But then, respecting this kind of initiative, they found him a White farm within the designated area of a homeland (called, rather curiously, a 'White spot'), which it bought out from the White farmer and turned over to him. He now not only operates this but has moved into other ventures, is a key figure in the organization of Black business-men called the African Chamber of Commerce, and has started a bank. He is full of missionary zeal about progress. Years ago I asked him:

What is your most urgent need?
Farmers' organizations! Until our people have farmers' organizations, that can teach them how to farm properly, we will never modernize our agriculture. And the reserves cannot be industrialized until agriculture is put on a sound footing.

This man is now one of a class of energetic Blacks who have moved forward under this same Government; who, seeing that the old themes of multiracial political agitation were leading them into a blank wall, have turned to economic activity as the only option open. They have recognized that the economic backwardness of the Black was not created by this Government or any previous government in South Africa. They further saw that as they advanced in the economic sphere, they would be able to make claims, as leaders of their people, that both protected and furthered this progress. This indeed happened. At the meeting held in January 1975 between the Prime Minister and the leaders of the Black homelands on the subject of the urban Blacks, all the familiar grievances were voiced: influx control, restrictions on Black traders, home-ownership, township amenities. On 1 May following, the Minister of Bantu Administration and Development announced that the position on home-ownership was to be restored to what it had been in 1967, namely 30-year leaseholds, which could be sold and bequeathed; he also made the following statement concerning trading rights:

... traders will also be permitted to trade in a larger range of commodities than at present, and also to establish more than one type of business on the same premises. Partnerships will also be allowed and where Bantu traders have already established businesses in a homeland, they will be permitted to retain their existing business in the urban residential area indefinitely. Building ownership, as mentioned in the case of houses, will again become possible for Bantu traders in the urban Bantu residential areas in the White areas in the same manner as in the case of houses.[61]

Shaken by the Soweto riots, the Government not only dropped a spurious qualification of homeland citizenship for home-ownership in urban areas, but opened up the right of freehold. On the assumption that this right will be fully actualized for both residential and commercial uses, there will be significant repercussions. It will be apparent that the main problem facing the Black traders is not the restrictions of the law or even a supply of capital. It is, rather, as they have told me themselves, the shortage of trained Black managerial personnel. This will have to be faced in a practical spirit. And so will the economic aspects of the homelands policy as a whole.

As one looks at the change, beginning from about 1970, which has been taking shape in South Africa regarding the present and the future of the Blacks, the word 'homelands' keeps coming up in public discussion over and over again. I talked several years ago to a Nationalist labour leader who had participated in a conference I attended on the wage gap. He did not have a very high opinion of the efficacy of the works committees permitted by the Government. In this respect he was a 'labour man'. When I then raised with him the question of union membership for Blacks, a pained expression came over his face. He began to give all kinds of reasons as to why this was impossible. Finally he said that, regardless of what he thought, this Government would not permit it in the near future. I then raised, almost in an abstract way, the possibility of working out some kind of labour voice for the Blacks via the homeland Governments that would be superior to the works committees. At once the pained look disappeared, and he replied that he was sure the solution lay along these lines, but without having any idea at all of what it was.

This is a kind of paradigm of the inner workings of ruling opinion in South Africa. The homeland idea became a panacea which seemed to solve all problems but in fact covered them up. To the extent that the implementation of the framework of homeland leadership has begun to free Whites from the fear of facing these problems, it has had a positive value in changing the atmosphere. In this new atmosphere what the Black leaders have been doing is to use their authority as spokesmen conferred upon them by the homeland idea to divest the latter of its utopian qualities. This means, exactly as Fagan recommended, normalizing the situation of the urban Blacks. It also means normalizing the status of the homelands. What are they really to become, economically as well as constitutionally? As noted earlier the independence of the Transkei was proclaimed in 1976. And Bophutatswana has now also declared its intention of following suit. But the Transkei is an old historic reserve dating from the time of the imperial administration, and is a relatively large and compact block of territory. The others are not now and never were of this character. They consist of scattered rural reserves interspersed by White-held land. As Paul Malherbe has shown in his trenchant analysis, *Multistan: A Way out of the South African Dilemma*, the problem of consolidating these is economically insurmountable, and this is true of many other aspects of the development policy at the present moment. There are, for example, too many growth points planned which South Africa cannot afford. He notes that, with the possible exception of Babelegi in the Tswana homeland, the location of the presently designated growth points is such that they will never be able to compete with existing growth points. Then too the race policy has led to a swollen civil service. Forty per cent of economically active Whites are employed by the State; and even if they are replaced by Blacks in the homelands, the fundamental economic facts of the situation would not be changed.[62]

In short the homelands project thus far is over-politicized, over-planned, over-bureaucratized. The thinking about it has been dominated by a reliance upon 'Investment Corporations' and 'Development Corporations' for the various ethnic units. These conceptions are a legacy of the Pact Government which, we recall, sought to make itself economically independent of Britain with the formation of an iron and steel industry by means of state capitalism (or socialism?). Leaving on one side the question of the efficiency or inefficiency of this statist enterprise, one is bound to note that the industrial revolution in South Africa had *begun* years before with a highly efficient mining industry, whose earnings were the substantial foundation of all later industrial growth, including that in the statist sector. We are also bound to note that the rapid development which has taken place in the private sector in South Africa has not been essentially disturbed or thwarted by growth in the statist sector. We need not bring into question the role of the state in performing economic functions which the private sector cannot or will not perform—granted that these too have costs—in order to question the relative superiority of the state versus the private sector in generating capital. And we may formulate this question in the most prosaic way. This is, which creates more new employment, a given amount of money in public expenditure or the same amount in private investment? In this respect Malherbe notes that there is more private South African investment in the independent state of Swaziland, which has placed no doctrinal obstacles upon such investment, than there is in all the Black homelands combined. And the difference this makes is manifest. On a different but related tack I should also mention what one Black businessman put to me, namely, 'Who needs the Bantu Investment Corporation today? We could go to a bank.'

The gist of the above criticism then is that the politicization or political interference with the forces of the market economy has deranged the economy, a criticism which is by no means unique to South Africa. While there is no businessman in South Africa who is unaware of the following, many people outside the country have little idea how explicitly the proponents of apartheid presented the doctrine as anti-*laissez-faire*, anti-'economic', anti-capitalist, anti- the interests of urban-based industry. This is not surprising, considering the origins of this policy in what Frankel has called 'the tyranny of economic paternalism'.[63] This has had several forms in South Africa. One of these, as we have noted, was the White-labour policy demanded by a politicized trade union movement. Having acquired political power, it could then force capital to make a pact with it on its own terms against the Black worker. The White-labour policy was, really, the South African equivalent of socialism. Both British trade unionists and Moscow-directed Communists supported this policy on the premise that the interest of capital lay in an ever-increasing supply of cheap, unskilled, migratory Black labour. Anyone who thinks that South Africa can be explained in Marxist terms is in the grip of a delusion equalled only by the belief that the law of supply and demand can be 'conquered' by technology.

Now to all the 'economic' criticisms of apartheid, which have been made not only ever since but even before this Government took power, the Nationalist theoreticians dug in with two massive points. The first was that any alternative would lead to the suicide of the White man. The second was an affirmation of faith. It could be formulated as 'where there's a will, there's a way.' In recent years this maxim has begun to lose credibility as the factor of costs, which could be politically concealed or wished away under the boom conditions that had prevailed in South Africa, returned. In this respect the career of the utopianism about the industrialization of the homelands will be not unlike that of the belief in Britain in nationalization as a panacea for all ills, or of the belief in the omnipotence of legislation to 'engineer' equality in the United States and Australia. So long as there is free public opinion, the question of costs (or who is going to pay for a programme) cannot be prevented from returning as a political factor. And South Africa is now facing something which can hardly fail to have a bearing on policy. This is the prospect of large-scale Black unemployment in the cities. South Africa can hardly avoid facing the fact, as carefully documented by Trevor Bell, that conflict can arise between politically planned industrial decentralization and economic growth.[64]

As for the situation of the Blacks in the urban areas, there is very little to say that was not in principle clearly delineated by the Report of the Fagan Commission. The economic processes are moving in a direction which the overall policy-makers of the country, instead of openly supporting, would like to pretend did not exist. There is now, for example, the nucleus of a Black managerial class in South Africa.

To conclude this chapter, two facts may be cited which bring the contemporary situation into relief. The first is that in the past four years *ad hoc* committees for Coloured Affairs and Indian Affairs of the City Council of Johannesburg were established. These consist in each case of equal numbers of Whites and Coloureds or Indians. These management committees, which are free to discuss anything, work well; and the curious thing is that the Coloured members, for example, are just as 'anti-apartheid' as are the Coloureds on the Coloured Representative Council. Yet this alone does not prevent the *ad hoc* committee from functioning. Why not? Most simply, the Coloureds now have a say in the structure, and they trust the local officials concerned, in a way which was not true of the Coloured Representative Council. During this same period the central Government terminated the responsibility of the municipalities for the Black townships, that they until then had administered. The Government set up Bantu Affairs Administration Boards which were bureaucratic instruments, and in which Blacks had no representation.

The second fact is that after the Soweto riots of 1976, in which the buildings of the Bantu Affairs Administration Board, among other things, were set on fire by a mob, it became immediately apparent how irrelevant the homeland leaders were in this crisis. The Government instinctively reached out to make contact with the urban leaders or the men on the spot. In fact the Minister of Bantu Affairs did not summon them to Pretoria but prudently went to Soweto himself to confer with these leaders. The issue which initially triggered the riots, the language of instruction in schools, which had been heating up for a month and about which officials in the Government had been warned, was easily and quickly resolved by the Minister. But if there had been adequate consultation in the first place, it never would have arisen as an issue, not to mention the more fundamental grievances at work.

The question facing South Africa is nothing other than whether the Government will draw the correct inferences from this story, which press upon the very nerve of the tensions between the *verkramptes* and the *verligtes* in the National Party. Without making any predictions one way or the other, it suffices to point out in conclusion that the constitutional problem in South Africa cannot even begin to be settled without dealing with what has now indisputably come to be the most urgent problem in the country. This, to repeat, is the absence of a consultative voice for the permanently settled Black townsmen. In making what is most urgent the naturally highest political priority, the Government would discover that the constitutional question of the relationship between the homeland leadership and the Government would settle itself.

III

The Social Framework

The social question is concerned at its core with marriage and friendship, or intimate association in private life. The fact that it is concerned with the private sphere does not make it politically indifferent, or indifferent to the character of a regime. It matters in a society composed of different ethnic groups whether these groups live together or separately. If the latter, it also matters whether they share a common way of life or not. Then too the social question can, as we see, become politicized. Thus politics can come to regulate, not only the right of ethnic intermarriage, but association in the public sphere which is not in any direct way concerned with intimate association.

The career of the social question under the regime of the Nationalist Government is not unlike that of the political question, with which it became intertwined. An extremist government came into power, pandering to certain opinions, prejudices, and fears at the expense of the politically weak groups. It then had to face up to the task of moderating or moving away from the originally negative dimension of its policy, while carrying the public opinion in its own party with it.

In this chapter, we shall examine the movement that is taking place in this sphere. In looking at both the direction and limits of change, we shall see how the social question parallels the political question.

Compulsory or voluntary separation?

The social question did not become drawn into South African politics because of intermarriages between cosmopolitan artists and intellectuals. The cause rather was the urbanization of the poor-Whites in the 1930s. As these people came into the cities, they gravitated to the cheapest housing available, which was either near or in non-White neighbourhoods. The Nationalists then made rhetorical capital out of racial friction and the danger of miscegenation in areas where Coloured and White were living 'cheek by jowl'. And, indeed, both being Afrikaans-speaking, they were not culturally estranged from each other. In any event an issue had emerged which could not be swept under the rug. As soon as the Purified Nationalists split from Hertzog, Dr. Malan began to exploit this issue in a demagogic way, needling Hertzog that 'he had no Coloured policy'. This was a political way of saying that he had a *laissez-faire* attitude to miscegenation. Finally, in answer to these accusations, Hertzog in March 1939 produced a statement of policy about the Coloured people which addressed itself, among other things, to the urban residential question. The essentials of his policy were identical to those which he had stated in his Smith-field speech in 1925. These were the political and industrial integration of the Coloureds throughout the Union on the one hand, and social separation on the other. With regard to the latter it is important to contrast the spirit and intention behind Hertzog's policy with what came later, and the difference it would have made in the way it was carried out:

Social Status.—There is no desire on the part of either the White or the Coloured people that there shall be social intercourse between them, and social separation is accepted by both as the definite and settled policy of the country. Wherever social or economic conditions conflicting with this policy of social separation are found to exist, the Government will do its best to remedy such conditions, but it will always try to do so in a manner that will avoid causing ill-feeling or a sense of grievance, and will involve no greater discrimination than the necessities of the case require.

The most effective step in this direction is the provision of adequate housing accommodation so that White and Coloured need not crowd together under slum conditions where it is difficult for the inhabitants to remain socially apart. This step has already been taken and with universal approval. The Government intends to go forward with this policy.[1]

The rest of Hertzog's statement concerns the question of the legislation he thought necessary to carry this out, the question of mixed residential areas which, he contended, existed only to a small extent, and the question of whether legislation to prevent mixed marriages, which he stated were looked upon with the greatest disfavour by both Whites and non-Whites, was likely to be desirable or effective. He deferred the last point to a commission as politicians characteristically do when they want to fend off a demagogic hot potato. In his concluding paragraph he stated:

The Government feels that the policy enunciated above is one in which both

Europeans and non-Europeans can co-operate, as it is designed to give effect
to the wish of both for social separation while avoiding any features that may
damage the material interests or hurt the feelings of either section.[2]

Whether Hertzog found it distasteful to be politically pushed into
making even this public statement, in which he rhetorically bent over
backwards to avoid insulting the Coloureds, is something one can
speculate about for oneself. As one may readily imagine, the Coloureds
themselves would regard with the greatest suspicion any statement by
a prime minister even hinting at compulsory segregation. The Indians,
in depositions before the Indian Penetration Commission, had been
quite explicit in saying that while in fact they preferred to live among
themselves, they objected to compulsory segregation laws, which they
obviously did not have a say in drawing up.[3] Booker T. Washington
had made the same point in 1915.[4]

Still, there was the agitation facing Hertzog about racial mixing in
the slums, which no South African politician could dismiss or ignore
without elevating its political importance. The question is, given the
spirit and intention indicated in Hertzog's statement, how would his
policy have been applied and with what effects? If his words be taken
at face value, new housing would have been earmarked for Coloureds
and Whites, in consultation with Coloured leaders. People then would
have moved voluntarily out of the slums as they were gradually cleared;
and self-segregation would have emerged as a by-product of the whole
process. The actualization of such a framework, going with rather than
against the interests of both the Coloureds and the Whites, would have
then undercut any further agitation about 'racial mixing'. Middle-class
Coloureds who had been living in mixed neighbourhoods all their lives
without 'racial friction' would have remained undisturbed and free to
stay where they were, or to move into middle-class Coloured areas as
these came into being. (It is improbable that freedom of choice would
have gone beyond this.) The actualization of this framework would
have also clipped the wings of demands for such laws as came later, like
the Immorality Act and the Prohibition of Intermarriage Act.

The War obviously prevented the United Party Government (now
under Smuts) from giving any priority to new housing schemes. And
when the Nationalists came in, they did indeed have an aggravated
housing problem on their hands, particularly among urban Blacks.
The law, however, which they enacted to deal with urban housing
was called the Group Areas Act. This was projected as part of the
policy of apartheid or total separation; and animated by the narrow
nationalism that elevated the self-preservation of the politically

dominant group into an unqualified goal, the whole purpose of the Act became distorted. Separation was for the sake of the Whites; and with the doctrinaire slogan that 'all racial mixing makes for racial friction', *regardless of the context*, the administration of the Act could hardly avoid injuring the interests of the non-Whites in both material and non-material ways. Groups which had been living as settled communities in the kinds of voluntary ethnic areas which arise in every large city were forced to relocate large distances from where they worked. Not only were they relocated against their wishes but they were faced with extra expenses for commuting. The removal of 'Black spots' became a slogan which then became the basis for triumphant announcements that another 'Black spot' had been removed. But as Fagan pointed out, what virtue was there in the purely ideological combination of a number of small 'Black spots' into one large one?[5] Furthermore, the location of Indian businesses, which had nothing to do with social separation, was pulled into the Group Areas Act, to the disadvantage of Indian businessmen.

The best indication of the spirit originally behind this Act is the fact that of the 63,314 families who were resettled after having been declared disqualified occupants of their houses, only 1,246 were White.[6] This went hand in hand with the imposition by law of segregation in public places, where it either had been conventional or had never existed. In the creation of amenities for the various races the standard of separate but equal was ruled to be not legally enforceable by the courts.

In fact most of the housing now standing in the group areas proclaimed under this Act is new housing built after the Act. In this respect it did indeed function as a slum clearance act. Where this objective, rather than 'separation for the sake of separation', grabbed hold of the administrators concerned, and when the non-Whites were effectively consulted, the administration of the Act began insensibly to partake of the spirit behind Hertzog's policy. Much later, a curious interchange was to take place in Parliament, with the Opposition saying, 'Why didn't you enact a slum clearance act as is done in normal countries?' and Government spokesmen replying, 'Why don't you give us credit for what we have done?' In the meantime the *verkramptheid* in the constituencies were accusing the Government of spending too much money on non-White housing. It is dubious whether the Government with its *verkrampte* power base could have passed an explicit slum clearance act, even if it had wanted to. The crucial point, however, is that in those cases where the administration of the Act was *verlig*

JOHANNESBURG
GROUP AREAS 1976

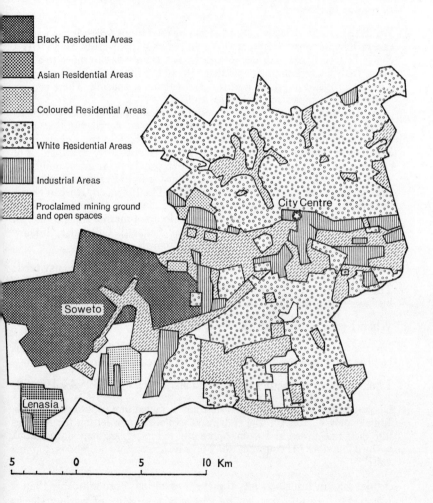

Black Residential Areas

Asian Residential Areas

Coloured Residential Areas

White Residential Areas

Industrial Areas

Proclaimed mining ground
and open spaces

City Centre

Soweto

Lenasia

5   0   5   10 Km

(which meant precisely to move *back* to Hertzog's intention), there was, not surprisingly, satisfaction on the part of the non-Whites. An Indian businessman in Durban, whom I interviewed in 1970, and who lived in an older house near his place of business, indicated this much in drawing up, so to speak, a balance-sheet of the Indian situation. While a number of things have since changed for the better, this statement is of historical interest because of what was already apparent to him even then:

We Indians in Durban are not so harried by the Group Areas Act as was the case in Johannesburg because we have a number of group areas. So we have a choice in accordance with our means. In fact I am going to move to a new house fairly soon. You must note that 75% of the Indians in Natal are poor. The Government has done a great deal for them in housing. There is a big Soweto-type complex in Durban for Indians.

We are harried by the fact that permits are required for inter-provincial travel. It was worse before but our Council has been working on this and it has ceased somewhat now. [These restrictions, except in the Orange Free State, were abolished in June 1975]. There is also petty apartheid. For example, there are lifts for Europeans only in certain government buildings, which require Indians to walk upstairs. Exclusion from European restaurants and cinemas does not particularly bother me. The Indians in Durban have a thriving night life with cinemas and night clubs and do not crave social mixing. Social integration with Europeans does not mean a thing to me. In the house I insist that the children speak Gujarati. Of course, I know perfectly well that outside they speak only English.

I then asked him what were the main things he wanted. He answered:

The end of university apartheid, freedom to travel, freedom to locate a business where we want, and the end of sport apartheid.

When I asked him about the vote, he said:

No, that is not so important now. But I'll tell you one thing. If the Indians had the vote, they would never vote for an African government.

I then asked him whether he ever had any contact with Blacks. He said:

Oh yes, I know an African lawyer here and I invited him to address our club. Immediately he attacked the Indians as exploiters, not letting the Africans into their businesses, and so on. So we said to him, 'Look man, do you think we own our stock? If you want to set up a business as we do, who is stopping you?'

As the Indian informed me, the evening ended more amicably than it began. He also told me that he knows of a number of trading Blacks who are being financed by Indian wholesalers.

In comparing the sentiments expressed above with the voluntary self-segregation (or self-enclosure) of White ethnic groups in South Africa—Jews, Greeks, Portuguese, Italians—and of ethnic groups generally in urban settings, one might be tempted to conclude that if only this were wholly voluntary it would be legitimate. For this would put White and non-White ethnic groups on the same legal plane. The fact is, however, that the White groups do not have a legally differentiated status but the non-Whites do. Among other things the present and the future of local government in South Africa are connected with this framework of separate residential communities which administer their own educational and social services. Furthermore, these communities are constituencies for elections to the separate ethnic councils. It is highly unlikely that this system will be dismantled in the near future. Thus it is impractical or academic to deal with the question of legal differentiation as if one were starting *de novo*. But then the question still remains of whether the legal differentiation is applied in such a way as to go with or against the sentiments of the people, or to support or thwart their own moral inclinations. The Theron Commission, while noting the 'widespread and intense opposition among the vast majority of Coloureds to the provisions and administration of the Group Areas Act', in fact concluded that the existence of separate residential areas and communities was so part of the basic pattern of the society that its structure could not be disturbed. It did, however, recommend certain changes in the Act. To begin with, it recommended that District Six in Cape Town be restored to the Coloureds. This is a section within the inner city of Cape Town that had been a Coloured area for generations, but which had been proclaimed a White area under the policy of rehousing all non-Whites in areas peripheral to the central city. The Theron Commission also recommended that a number of radical adjustments would have to be made regarding commercial opportunities and entertainment and recreational facilities:

(a) with a view to the more satisfactory regulation of the social relations and opportunities for contact between members of the various population groups, as well as the creation of more equitable opportunities for entrepreneurs of the population groups concerned, the Group Areas Act be amended so that certain areas (namely, specific concentrated business and industrial areas) may be demarcated as UNCONTROLLED areas, i.e. that members of the population groups concerned to whom these areas have been opened will, in terms of the Group Areas Act, qualify in these areas as 'qualified persons' as regards land-ownership and occupation;
(b) with a view to opening up a greater choice in the use of entertainment and recreational facilities, the Groups Areas Act be so amended that a local authority, on application by the owner or person in control of such a facility,

may generally authorize the use thereof by members of other population groups even though such facility is situated in a proclaimed group area.[7*]

Finally one must note that the Theron Commission forthrightly recommended that the statutory prohibitions on mixed marriages and carnal intercourse between White and non-White be repealed as a 'racist' stigma and in order 'to promote the accepted policy-objective of moving away from discrimination on grounds of race or colour'.[8] The Government rejected this recommendation.

The clearest example showing that the practical issue is not simply legal differentiation in the abstract is the case of the urban Blacks. These people have faced an overall legal structure which sought to define them as transients or casuals and which as such was in tension with the inclinations of the people themselves to generate a normal ethnic community. That the law was never applied in such a way, by this or any previous government in South Africa, as to block this out of existence, should be made emphatically clear. It is seen in, among other things, the trend towards normality in the sex ratio over the years, notwithstanding the relatively recent introduction of single-sex hostels.

Table 22: Sex ratios of the Black population, Johannesburg Metropolitan Area, 1911–70

Census year	Males per 100 females
1911	2 240·4
1921	771·4
1936	273·5
1946	176·8
1951	147·8
1960	117·6
1970	110·2

Source: Non-European Affairs Department, Johannesburg.

Note: Changes in the metropolitan boundary during the period 1911–70 are not significant for the above figures.

* Not surprisingly the Commission divided on these recommendations. The minority contended that they 'amounted to the systematic dismantling of separate development in general and the Group Areas Act in particular'. In the South African rhetorical context one might reply that it is not a question of 'dismantling' separate development as of humanizing it or of making it work in a way that carries sentiment and opinion with it. Perhaps nothing brings out the true difference between *verkramptheid* and *verligtheid* more clearly than the division on this issue. It is in fact the age-old distinction between 'separation for the sake of separation' and separation in those respects and in those modes where it subserves the requirements of justice.

If the law, however, did not block the movement towards a normal community, its harassments are not to be minimized either. In the present context we should note how the law can interfere with efforts that people in the community were prepared to make to help themselves. A former leader of the elected Urban Bantu Council in Johannesburg put it clearly:

We accept the idea of a Bantu residential community. We are not worried about it as 'segregation'. What we want, however, is security and the freedom to develop the community.

To give one example of the problems that these Black urban leaders face, the Council several years ago voted to levy a tax that the Blacks themselves would pay out of their own pockets towards an additional secondary school in Soweto. The Department of Bantu Affairs at once stated that this was contrary to policy and that additional secondary schools should be located in the homelands. As a result of continual pressure by the Blacks, and financial support by the Whites in Johannesburg, this situation has changed somewhat. I would expect this to change even more in the future. But for the moment one must emphasize the fact, not only for its practical but also its theoretical implications, that so long as the law fears any manifestation of 'permanence', it collides with the interests of the hard-working small property holders, who have a stake in the community and a stake in law and order. Thus it unintentionally favours the lawless, who plague the large urban townships and prey on their inhabitants, who know how to forge and buy passes, and who would be a problem under any conditions. The settled Black townsmen in Johannesburg understandably want the system of migratory labour on one-year contracts discontinued. They have made representations to the Government asking that the hostels for the unattached migratory male workers be not located near the areas of home-owners, which as they put it was just 'asking for trouble':

There are very rough people here in Soweto. I had to burglar-proof the windows of the stockroom of the garage to protect it. I was once held up, when I lost 900 Rand. Now I use an armoured service. If we businessmen were in control of the townships, we could put a stop to this. Some of the police are in cahoots with the criminals. The gangsters live during the day in houses unmolested.

As noted in the previous chapter the Government finally modified policy about home-ownership in the urban areas. The question arises as to whether home-ownership will be the privilege of a small élite

5

who are envied and resented. In fact right now 30% of the houses in the urban townships are owned under the system discontinued in 1967.[9] The expansion of the Black middle class in this direction will obviously generate a stable majority and put ground under its feet in setting the moral tone of the community.

Then too, once Blacks can put up land as collateral in borrowing from commercial banks, they can expand their businesses. The Government, to be sure, has always provided an array of public amenities; but these townships are still huge dormitory cities without the vitality of a 'downtown', Soweto, a Black city which may unofficially have a population of $1\frac{1}{2}$ millions, has for long had only two cinemas. The liberation of Black (and also non-Black) private enterprise from the restrictions under which it has operated could thus inject vitality and facilities into these townships. The Black middle-class housewife, for example, does not buy from the traders in the townships, whose prices are not competitive. Like her White counterpart, she drives her car to a supermarket, 'in town'. This enterprise could also play a role in alleviating the housing shortage and improving the quality of the housing in these communities. Private enterprise contends that it could provide electrification for Soweto in less than half the time that the West Rand Bantu Administration Affairs Board has projected for this long overdue service.

Finally, one should mention the law concerning freedom of personal movement. The Coloureds and the Indians (with two exceptions) now have freedom to move and to settle throughout the whole of the country without restrictions. The Blacks do not. They are subject to influx control, and are required to obtain statutory permission to work and to reside in an urban area; all this is a very bureaucratized procedure. The Blacks in Johannesburg persevered in making representations to get free movement of Black labour within the greater Witwatersrand metropolitan area. This consists of separate municipalities, each of which has its own influx control office; and to the gratification of the Black leaders, the situation in this respect was simplified and eased. The familiar justification for influx control is that without such regulation, the urban areas would be inundated by people from the rural areas who with very low living standards would be prepared to squat in makeshift housing.* What is undisputable, however, is that the Pass Laws, the infraction of which was a criminal offence, fell equally and in the most undifferentiated way upon the shoulders of the settled

* When the restrictions on the inter-provincial movement of Indians were abolished, there was no 'mass influx' of poor Indians from Natal to the Transvaal.

Table 23: Urban population in selected cities, by race, 1951, 1960, and 1970

A.
(Figures in thousands)

	Total	Whites	Coloureds	Asians	Blacks[a]
Johannesburg					
1951	919	366	39	22	492
1960	1 153	413	60	29	651
1970	1 433	501	83	39	810
Cape Town					
1951	632	267	297	8	60
1960	807	305	418	9	75
1970	1 097	379	599	11	108
Durban					
1951	498	153	18	166	162
1960	654	196	27	235	197
1970	843	258	44	317	225
Pretoria					
1951	285	151	6	6	122
1960	423	207	8	8	200
1970	561	305	11	11	235

B.
(percentages)[b]

	Total	Whites	Coloureds	Asians	Blacks
Johannesburg					
1951	100	39·8	4·2	2·4	53·5
1960	100	35·9	5·2	2·5	56·5
1970	100	35·0	5·8	2·7	56·5
Cape Town					
1951	100	42·2	47·0	1·3	9·5
1960	100	37·8	51·8	1·1	9·3
1970	100	34·5	54·6	1·0	9·8
Durban					
1951	100	30·7	3·5	33·2	32·6
1960	100	29·8	4·1	35·9	30·1
1970	100	30·6	5·2	37·6	26·7
Pretoria					
1951	100	53·0	2·1	2·1	42·9
1960	100	49·0	1·8	1·9	47·3
1970	100	54·3	2·0	2·0	41·9

Sources: Statistical Abstract, 1966, p. A—25, and Bulletin Statistics, March 1972, Dept. of Statistics, Pretoria, Table A2.0, p. 3, for 1960 and 1970 figures.

Notes: (a) The probability of the figures for the Black urban population being under-estimated is high. This is due in part to the possibly large number of illegal Blacks (i.e. without valid passes for urban residence) who avoid census and survey enumeration.

(b) Some of the percentage shifts in population groups between the census years are due to boundary changes in the metropolitan areas.

townsmen and migratory workers, genuine work-seekers and criminal floaters, etc. Thus it has been the sorest bone of contention among the Blacks, more so in fact than the absence of the vote. One may recall the 1947 statement of Councillor Thema quoted earlier.[10] The Fagan Commission looked into the question of the Pass Laws. It did not recommend that all regulation of internal migration be abolished, given the disparity in cultural standards not merely between Black and White, but also between Black and Black. It did, however, recommend ways in which the Pass Laws could be humanized to serve the interests of all concerned. To begin with, it completely disconnected the objective of regulation from the fallacious economic assumptions underneath the apartheid policy. Regulation was to have the function, by the institution of labour bureaux, of helping work-seekers find work, and employers find labour.[11] The Fagan Commission also unambiguously stipulated that Blacks themselves sit on committees concerned with the regulation of this internal migration. The Government has now proposed something in this direction as an outcome of a recent meeting between the Prime Minister and the homeland leaders. The problem has by no means been resolved. And the consultation that has thus far taken place is not that kind of open, bi-partisan consultation, covered by the press, which Fagan saw as a requirement of effective consultation. But we may perhaps call what is going on now the end of the beginning of this age-old grievance.

Beyond the ethnic chessboard

The gist of the previous section is that what is fundamentally at issue in South Africa is not the legal framework of separate ethnic communities. In fact, no political party in South Africa could repudiate this framework and propose to start again from scratch. Even the Progressives in the 1974 election had finally come to accept the framework of Bantu territorial authorities in the rural areas, which they had for long opposed as contradictory to their standard of a common franchise. Among other reasons for this shift in White opinion is that the non-Whites themselves became involved in this framework. They began to acquire a stake in it as something that they could not merely live with but use for their benefit. Thus the real issue, to repeat, is the quality of life in these communities. To go somewhat further we could say that this issue is whether these communities are alienated from each other with conflicting standards and resentments, steeped in inequality, or whether they share in fundamental respects a common way of life. Let us first consider how this issue was complicated by rhetoric.

When the Nationalist Government came into power, it allied itself with a doctrine which had been voiced in South Africa for decades, and not only by Afrikaner nationalism. We had seen it articulated in the *Report of the Native Economic Commission 1930–32*. This doctrine was that the educated Black was a marginal man, an *évolué* who was in between two worlds. By virtue of his education, he had contempt for the traditional culture of his own people. And yet he was not socially accepted by European or White society either. Thus, like all marginal men, he was frustrated from every side and would inevitably become a destructive agitator, voicing not the real needs of his people but his own personal *ressentiment*. People then drew the inference that if the politics of destruction and *ressentiment* were to be nipped in the bud, the educated Black must be encouraged, indeed forced, to go back to his own people, among whom he would become a natural teacher and leader. He could therefore play a constructive role in their movement towards the very same civilization to which he had opened himself and which he could never repudiate, granted that the movement of the people as a whole would be 'along their own lines'. This last phrase was admittedly vague. It seemed to some to mean cultural stagnation. It could also have meant in a practical respect using traditional social and political institutions as a basis for progressive change, rather than confronting them in the spirit of making a clean sweep.

A parallel argument was projected about the Coloureds. It could not be identical since the Coloureds did not have a distinct language. The thesis here was to regard the Coloureds collectively as *évolués*. They were in between the Blacks and the Whites. Because of both colour prejudice and their Westernized way of life, they could not fuse either with the Blacks or with the Whites. This marginality only inflamed the desire of those who could do so to pass for White, which was eating the soul out of the Coloured people. The remedy? Force them to develop an ethnic pride of their own and even to recognize their distinct 'culture', and they would get rid of their inferiority complex.

On this basis the Government moved to implement its policy in ways which went far beyond merely residential separation. We limit ourselves here to two points anticipated above. The first is that the Government turned to the traditional chiefs in fashioning the framework of the Bantu Authorities. The second is that it categorically terminated the right of all non-White students—with certain exceptions at the discretion of the Government—to enroll at those White universities which had formerly accepted them, and established separate university colleges for Blacks, Coloureds, and Indians.

To these developments the liberal opposition in South Africa reacted in ways which were not surprising. To begin with, it saw the justifications of the policy as self-serving rhetoric to cloak and sweeten the fact of White supremacy, or as punitive racial discrimination. Then too it saw the policy as leading to Black power, an inflammation not merely of anti-White racial hatred but a spurious form of cultural nationalism as well. Chieftainship was seen as reactionary, in fact as reactionary as Reitz thought it was. And as for the university colleges set up for the non-Whites, these became immediately dubbed 'tribal colleges'.

As with everything else in South Africa that is publicly stated, one must get beyond the dimension of rhetoric and counter-rhetoric to look at the facts sociologically. I entitled this section 'Beyond the Ethnic Chessboard'. This is an obvious parallel to the phrase 'beyond the melting pot' that Glazer and Moynihan coined to describe the ethnic framework of the United States.[12] There, in the face of an overwhelmingly assimilationist self-understanding of the society, one could see that assimilation, in the sense of fusion or total absorption through intermarriage, had only taken place among those non-English stocks from Northern Europe who, in both racial and religious respects, were similar to the original Anglo-American colonists. Even here, however, where the groups were sufficiently numerous and compact they did not necessarily lose their ethnic identity, as shown by the voting behaviour of Germans and Scandinavians in Minnesota during both World Wars.[13] But certainly among immigrants of these stocks complete absorption did occur, as shown by such names as Roosevelt and Eisenhower, who would hardly have been regarded as less than '100% American' by anyone except the Nazis. In South Africa, the Huguenots were totally absorbed by the Afrikaners with a loss of their French ethnic identity. Their French names survive, but in South Africa they are socially perceived as Afrikaner names.

Where, however, there was a racial or religious barrier or prejudice against intermarriage, the groups did not 'melt' but persisted. This social prejudice against absorption is a form of social inequality, however much it is reciprocated by all concerned. Yet, as Glazer and Moynihan pointed out, the barrier was not in the successful cases an obstacle to assimilation. And assimilation, in practical respects, comprehends the enjoyment of an overriding equality in the public sphere, including the occupational structure. Why? Very simply, the groups assimilated collectively as groups. While the ethnic group continues to be a focus of social attachment, the group as a whole 'evolves'. And where this takes place, the problem of the isolated *évolué* becomes academic. They don't want you in their club. You form your own and stop whining. This is not as perfect a solution of the ethnic problem as assimilation by way of fusion. But it can be lived with and lived with well, so much so that people would resent social pressure to forsake their ethnic identity and cease being 'clannish'.[14]

In South Africa exactly the same process is taking place but from a different direction. There the regnant standpoint was formed over centuries by the spectacle, not of immigrants arriving from Europe who were needed to clear the land, but of the co-presence of native tribes. And yet what are the facts? Anthropologists in South Africa have richly documented the process of acculturation among Blacks in their movement from tribal life into the urban areas.[15] They have shown the social bifurcation which exists in the township. At one pole are the 'tribesmen', who resist change. Among other reasons they are fearful of the demoralization which occurs among those of their kin who abandon the traditional restraints of the tribal customs and fail to get attached to those solid goals which modern bourgeois life supplies. These then become not *évolués* but *tsotsis* (criminals). At the other pole are the 'townsmen', who have made a much more profound inner change. Yet even among the latter traditional customs such as *lobola* or bride-price persist, but their content is adapted to city life. Even the languages are in a peculiar flux, especially among the educated. I asked such a Black:

What language do you speak at home?
To tell the truth I find it hard to say. We can begin a sentence in one language and end it in another. This goes on all the time.

Among the settled townsmen this process of acculturation or communal assimilation is seen in the expanding network of voluntary associations. An important sphere in this respect is religion.[16] The Blacks in South Africa as in America have a thriving church life, much of which is organized in autonomous or separatist bodies, which are huge in number. In Soweto alone there are over 900 independent churches. In the White residential areas one can commonly see domestic servants who are attached to these separatist denominations congregating for services in vacant lots. The leaders of the separatist federations are charismatic individuals, some of whom have a lot of money at their disposal and have put it to work in enterprises along the lines of Father Divine. The educated Black does not participate in religious life on this level and belongs to regular religious denominations which have Black affiliates or branches. While in the social life of the educated Black, kinship still plays a large role, there are also voluntary organizations of a non-religious character. And a stratification of society has emerged based not upon kinship but upon education, life-style, and conspicuous consumption. Several years ago the Blacks in Soweto had their first 'Debutantes' Ball'.[17]

How does this whole process of assimilation as a group look from the perspective of those partaking in it? I quote two citations from interviews. The first was with a laundress whom I employed in Johannesburg:

Veronica, how is it that you speak English so well and Charlie speaks it so badly, and yet you are both Zulus?
Oh, thank you very much. Well, in the part of Natal where I come from there are many Europeans, so it was easy to pick up the language. But where Charlie comes from there are very few Europeans. The women there still walk around like this [pointed to her breasts].

The second was with the Indian businessman quoted earlier. The Indians, one must note, were described in the 1947 statement on Race Relations of the National Party as a 'foreign element which cannot be assimilated in the South African set-up'.[18] To be sure they are Muslim or Hindu, have different marriage customs, maintain separation of sexes at meals, and the Indian women wear Indian dress, although the occasional Indian woman is seen in Western dress. The Indians also eat Indian cuisine in their homes, though, as my informant told me, 'not for breakfast'. I asked him:

Do you have any contact with India?
Yes. I—but not my children—keep in touch with my relations in India. I went to visit them some time ago and was shocked by their standard of living, which was much lower than ours, even though they are much richer. For example, they ate on the floor. Later on, an Indian relation returned the visit and expected us somehow to be living on a low scale. He thought that our businesses would be tiny shops like in India. To his amazement he discovered that we lived in a nice house with good furniture and ate on tables. And from that moment he resolved that he too would eat on a table! The Indians in South Africa are much more westernized than those in India. I did not feel at home in India.

To juxtapose the main points of the previous section and of this section thus far, the operation of a social tendency towards two not irreconcilable goals is seen. The first goal is the persistence of ethnic communities. The second is what may be called a framework of bourgeois order and liberty. From this it might seem axiomatic that a government which dealt with the prejudices and sentiments precipitating the first goal so as to strengthen and maximize the second would achieve the greatest degree possible of prosperity and tranquillity. This may be true, but there is certainly no historical necessity that prudence will rule, to look no further than Northern Ireland. Over and above the force of national sentiments and passions, the politics of this century have been permeated by doctrines of both the right and the left, which simultaneously inflame and pander to these passions, while assaulting the validity of this solution and, indeed, of reason itself. Furthermore, the adherents of these doctrines have been able to establish regimes within which they are able to exempt themselves from the verdict of experience. They do this by controlling public opinion and the right of emigration, and by intensive propaganda blaming the regimes they are attacking for their failures while passing the buck to history.

All this remains true, and I shall return to what is really the problem of constitutional democracy in the final chapter. But for the time being it suffices to point out that however politically successful these regimes based on these doctrines are, in not simply holding on to but in aggrandizing their power, we cannot underestimate either the success which a government that encourages and protects the operation of this social tendency towards the two different goals can have in resisting these doctrines. This, in fact, supplies *the* intelligible standard for seeing where South Africa has succeeded and where it has blundered. This can be seen, not only in the economic situation, but also with regard to the two points noted at the outset of this section, namely chieftainship and the establishment of the ethnic universities, both of which, one will recall, collided with received opinion.

As for the first, the essentials are amazingly simple. Where the chiefs are educated men who supported this social tendency, as are all the heads of the homeland Governments, they are respected by townsmen and tribesmen alike. Hence, they are a bridge between the two wings of Black society. As educational leaders in the rural areas they are agents of assimilation who know both the score and how to talk to their people. Where on the other hand the subordinate chiefs and headmen were uneducated men put on government payrolls to support the Bantu Authorities Act, the results were as one might expect. Consider the following comments:

Chief A—— was very progressive. He was interested in schools and modern agriculture unlike many chiefs. His son is a student. Like many of our young boys he drinks too much. Chief A—— was not one who was always crying. He accepted the Bantu Authorities for progressive purposes. He taught the people to rotate their cattle and also to get rid of the animals like donkeys which are useless today but overgraze the land.

Also:

Chief B—— is not just a politician. He is also very keen on modern farming. If he is driving in his car and sees someone doing something wrong, he will stop and give the person a good talking to. In one case he had a whole lorry-load of manure dumped right on the front doorstep of someone who was abusing the land.

But on the other side:

There are illiterates on the African advisory boards. Even on the Bantu Education Advisory Board there are uneducated chiefs to whom the most elementary things have to be explained and which holds up the discussion.

Also:

If they have the same calibre of man in the Urban Bantu Councils that they do on the Territorial Authorities, they will be useless. We have chiefs on our Territorial Authority who cannot read a balance sheet. The result is that money which is allocated for the Authority is unexpended and returned.

The Government, one must note, established a school for the sons of chiefs and headmen when it began to implement the framework of Bantu Authorities; and it may be surmised that the uneducated chief will disappear from the administrative framework over the ensuing years.

As for the ethnic university colleges, these, to repeat, were established by legislation which simultaneously excluded the non-Whites from the White universities. This soured the atmosphere at the time and gave rise, as noted, to the epithet 'tribal colleges'. This term has disappeared among Blacks who began to regard it as an insult not to the Government but to them.* These institutions, which are all held to the standards of the University of South Africa, began to be seen in a different light after Dr. Van der Ross, a distinguished Coloured educator and an articulate critic of racial discrimination, was appointed to the rectorship of the Coloured University College of the Western Cape at Belleville. Blacks have also been demanding that they be

---

* I infer this from personal experience. I used the term 'tribal colleges' in talking to a Black who then said to me, 'Why do you call them tribal colleges?' This was in 1970.

appointed to equivalent positions; and a Black, Professor Kgware, has now been appointed to the rectorship of the University College of the North. The Government has begun to move away from the high-point of categorical segregation which existed at the moment of their institution. Non-Whites will in the future be able to enroll more normally for courses at the White universities which are not available at the ethnic universities. But even if all racial laws were abolished tomorrow, these institutions would continue to prosper as have the leading Black universities in the United States. (The weak ones there are in difficulties.) The Theron Commission recommended that all universities be thrown open to Coloured students (postgraduate and graduate); that the University of the Western Cape be permitted to enroll approved White students at postgraduate level; and that the selection of students for admission should be vested in the universities.[19] The University College for Indians at Westville has a specialization in Indian Studies which exists nowhere else in the country; and not surprisingly there are White postgraduate students pursuing these studies there. The Theron Commission also made the important recommendation that the University of the Western Cape be no longer administered by its appropriate ethnic department (i.e., Coloured Affairs):

Having regard to its (possible autonomous) status and common interests between the University of the Western Cape and other universities, the Commission recommends that:
the University of the Western Cape fall under the Department of National Education.[20]

Finally, we turn to the question of ethnic 'power', in cultural and political respects. Curiously, in South Africa it was the Government which took the lead in 'ethnicizing' the curriculum, not in the universities, but in the primary schools. The key point here was its imposition of the use of the various Black languages as the medium of instruction, instead of English or Afrikaans. This at once encountered the strongest objections from the Blacks themselves. The principal objection was that the use of the vernacular disadvantaged the students for further study. The matriculation examinations are in the White languages, the medium of instruction in the secondary schools is either English or Afrikaans, and in the three university colleges it is English. The Transkei Government, asserting itself in this respect, abolished, among its first acts of legislation, the vernacular as the medium of tuition above the lower grades of primary school, and the rest of South Africa will undoubtedly follow suit.

As for the modes of ethnic consciousness projected by intellectuals, this too exists in South Africa. One sign of this is that Black students declared that they no longer wish to be known as 'non-White' or even 'African' but rather as 'Black'. And by and large this term has begun to replace 'African', which had replaced the earlier term 'Native'. The term 'Bantu' was never accepted by the Blacks. Some students have also declared their opposition to having European first names. As elsewhere, there is a generation-gap in these matters of style. A Black woman in Johannesburg stated the following to me:

Since you were last here 'Black is beautiful' has definitely come to South Africa. You should see the wigs and the prices!
What about tribal identifications?
It's coming in a little bit. You can go to a party and a few of the women will drop one or two sentences or do something and say, 'That's part of our Tswana tradition.'
Are people wearing tribal costumes?
Ag, the other day a man came right out in this street (*in Soweto*) dressed as a Zulu warrior. The kids went absolutely wild about it. I suppose you can say he made it with them.

The Theron Commission, one must note, recommended that the idea that the Coloured population is a community which is culturally different and culturally distinguishable from the White population groups, be abandoned. Thus it recommended that the advancement and pursuit of Coloured culture be dealt with within the same organizational framework as for Afrikaans-speaking and English-speaking Whites in South Africa.[21]

As for the political manifestation of ethnic consciousness or of 'Black Power' in the recognizable usage of this term, this is another matter. Some years back there were disturbances at the University College of the Western Cape. For several years there have also been disturbances at the University of the North, the Black institution established at Turfloop where there is a militant branch of the South African Students' Organization (SASO). At one point the Government closed the University. Finally the Government appointed a one-man (Snyman) commission, which reported in February 1976, and which was appalled by the strong anti-White feeling it found among both the students and the Black staff of the University. The commission recommended that differences in salaries paid to White and Black be wiped out, that legislation be amended so that the university will be seen to be autonomous and be allowed to administer its own financial affairs, and that postgraduate students be allowed to study at any university in South Africa—Black or White. The commission also reported that

SASO's main aim was the promotion of hatred of Whites, the destruction of the universities for Blacks, and incitement to armed revolution. This Government has not and will not hesitate to use its police power against the propagation of revolutionary change, by either Black or White student organizations. And while the changes recommended by the Snyman Commission, when implemented, may alleviate the situation, these changes do not obviate the need for consultative machinery in the political system. Had moderate Black opinion been effectively consulted, it would have told the Government fifteen years ago the same thing it told the Snyman Commission. Such consultation would hardly have prevented the appearance of apocalyptic radicalism, namely, the view that one cannot improve the tiniest part of the system without first totally transforming the whole. This view, which is the standard fare of every coffee-house intellectual, has been, after all, an element in the politico-intellectual atmosphere of the West since the French Revolution. What such consultation would do, however, is to shore up the position of the moderates. It would do this by politically excising the inference that in order for them to be heard, radicals must first provoke the Government.

The public sphere

Many people, in looking at South Africa or similar societies from, so to speak, the bottom up, and seeing racial prejudices at work, conclude that until populist racialism is eradicated, there can be no movement towards equality. While it is undoubtedly true that if there were no racial prejudices, there would be no racial discrimination, this way of looking at the problem, however elegant theoretically, is practically misleading. In the first place it leaves unanswered the question of who is going to bell the cat or of how vulgar prejudice is to be changed. More than this, however, the assumption that there is a uniform or monolithic body of prejudice is a wrong one. This is so obvious that I almost hesitate to mention it. Yet the way in which the concept 'racialism' is used in contemporary thinking about race relations, seems to imply that nothing less than a kind of mass psychological transformation is prerequisite to any social change. Against this it may or may not be altogether useless to mention the banalities that people are different, and that they can change with new experiences. Hence, on the level of ordinary social interaction, there is no absolute uniformity. A senior government official, for example, said to me:

When I was a boy in the Northern Transvaal, it would have been beyond the wildest stretch of my imagination to think that a Bantu would ever walk into an office such as this dressed in a business suit.

Beyond the flux within private, social interaction, a purely psychological (or individualistic) approach must ignore the role of political authority in fixing, reinforcing, or changing what seem to be 'patterns' of prejudice. But people take cues from political authority. They do this because public authority, by its very constitution, can give to a pattern of behaviour a stamp of approval that no private person can confer. This authority is of course circumscribed within limits by the prejudices and opinions of the people. But, since these opinions contradict each other, they do not form a coherent, logical pattern.[22] This authority is not simply determined by these prejudices. It has a degree of freedom to act one way or another, the outcome of which will tend to fix a public standard of behaviour at that moment. This can either be in a positive or negative direction. Much of the petty apartheid, otherwise known as the 'pin-pricks', in South Africa, was an attempt to fix by law, in consonance with the doctrine of total separation, patterns of segregation in the public sphere which placated the *verkrampte* constituents of the Government but which other parts of public opinion did not vocally or universally demand.

Once, however, the Government had thrown down the gauntlet with its policy of 'total apartheid', the existence of any permitted integration in the public sphere, particularly if this were in the public spotlight, was capable of being seen as a challenge to this policy, or as an admission that it was bankrupt.[23] This was especially so in spheres where South Africa was subject to external pressures, such as in sport. Against all such pressures, Dr. Verwoerd rigidly laid down and held the line that there would be no mixed sports within the country.

As the political question began to settle after the completion of the framework of Bantu Authorities, and as the *verligtheid* in the National Party began to assert itself, things began to change. Mr. Vorster was aware of the fact that the New Zealand Government, which had not put any pressure on South Africa, had none the less laid down the terms that it would not send *its* national rugby team to South Africa in 1970 without its Maori players; and he reversed Dr. Verwoerd's policy. However, he so confounded this with rhetoric that, as I was informed, his own party did not fully know what he was doing. His reticence was understandable. As soon as it did become known, it at once became an issue during the 1970 election. The Herstigtes, as will be recalled, attacked the Government on the issues of the Maoris and the Black ambassadors. In any event the games took place without trouble. The Herstigtes vowed to boycott them. But it was difficult to get tickets. And since then there have been other changes in the rules governing sport, and in public amenities.

This whole process of normalization of the public sphere is now under way. Though it is far from complete, we can now begin to see the direction in which further change will take place, which is altogether different from what it was in the 1950s. What is politically of interest is how a government, when a large part of its electorate identified apartheid with Jim Crow, managed to reverse policy in response, not only to external pressures, but also to moral dictates, without upsetting its own apple cart. Obviously it would not have moved to make a change without identifiable support from within its own caucus and the party as a whole. The rhetorical ploy, of which the Government has made intensive use thus far, to impose *verligtheid* over the *verkramptheid* in the National Party, has been the distinction between 'national' and 'international'. Just as all non-White diplomatic personnel were exempted from the beginning from any legal racial discrimination, so has the Government moved to exempt all foreign visitors to the Republic from restrictions in hotels. It also moved to establish as 'international' a number of hotels and restaurants which are open to all races within South Africa. The same distinction, by the way, is also at work in what may appear to be the gyrations about sports policy. All this is only a beginning and by no means free of legalistic complications, as the debate on the desegregation of hotels showed.[24] It is also by no means free from the political attack that 'the fundamental policy of the country is being systematically dismantled'. Against this, as voiced by the majority recommendations of the Theron Commission, is the defence that this relaxation is what is demanded by the policy of 'non-discrimination'. In fact what is emerging as a practical centre position on these issues is the advancement of the policy of 'free choice'—the creation of spheres where people are free to associate with whomever they wish. For example, the Theron Commission explicitly recommended that scientific, professional, industrial, business, and similar interest organizations 'themselves (and without official directives and conditions)' should be able to decide whether or not they will admit Coloureds as well as Whites.[25] And what applies to Coloureds applies to all. This is the way in which the permeation of society in South Africa by politics will be gradually reduced.

IV

Fagan: Consent and Principle in a Constitutional Democracy

In the previous chapters I presented some of the main indications of the way in which South Africa has at last begun to moderate what was a very doctrinaire blueprint. In this final chapter I conclude with some general reflections about the character of this change. I shall do this by way of a restatement of the standpoint of the most thoughtful person who has discoursed upon the subject of race relations in South Africa, the late Chief Justice Fagan. Given the fact that his views were free of narrow partisanship, they are a more comprehensive guide to what has been happening and what is likely to happen in South Africa than the statements of any of the people in the heat of the political fray, whether in the Government or the Opposition. This is because, as I stated in Chapter I, Fagan's views constitute a standard for judging what is both possible and right. To begin with, Fagan, in a private letter written shortly after the Nationalists came to power, had a prescient insight about the course he thought South African public opinion would take over the ensuing years:

I am indeed sorry that our Report has become a ball in the political game. However, all things work together for the good. I take the result of the election to mean that the Government now has a mandate from the people to *try* at any rate to apply the policy of 'total territorial segregation' which our Commission considered to be impracticable. As a good citizen and democrat I submit to the people's mandate and accept the position that it is now the duty of the Government to try to carry it out. If the attempt succeeds, well and good. If not, it will nevertheless be a preparatory step—and one which would appear to be necessary—to bring the mentality of the public to maturity on the question and to get people to acquiesce in a policy which concedes the impossibility of total territorial segregation and regards our task as being to find the best way of adapting ourselves to what is possible. I myself, when I was busy with our Report and spoke to people who believed in the idea of total segregation, sometimes wished that the whole thing was a game in which I could say: 'You believe it can be done, I believe it cannot; let us try it, and after the attempt we may talk again.' Now Providence has so arranged matters that the attempt will be made; I consider that we should give it a fair chance and await the result with an open mind.[1]

In this letter we see Fagan conceding the point that the victory of the doctrinaire policy of total territorial segregation, which he continued to oppose for the rest of his life, might after all have been pedagogically useful. He even went so far as to suggest that it might have been necessary to explode the myth once and for all. He did not therefore regard 1948, at that moment, as a disaster that would irrevocably 'set back the clock'. Why not? Crucial for Fagan was the overpowering character of facts. Given the existence of a free public opinion, any regime which sought to do the impossible would sooner or later have to moderate its politics in the face of these facts. The unsettled questions, which had been smothered by rhetoric aimed at denying these facts, would, far from vanishing, become once again discussible in a sober way when the atmosphere had cleared.

In this respect Fagan's prediction was correct. This is shown most easily by the fact that no one today seriously talks about the possibility of a mass efflux of Blacks from the towns back to the homelands. Fagan's views are therefore as pertinent today as they were in 1948. It is of political interest, however, that his name has virtually disappeared from the forefront of public debate.* Why? Most simply, Fagan had a principled opposition to blueprint solutions of the franchise question, including those of the United Party, in which he eventually found a political home. Because of the taste for blueprint solutions that, while not created, was certainly accentuated by the Nationalist regime, any political proposal that did not culminate in such a solution became regarded as effeminate because it refused 'resolutely' to face the ultimate questions. Or else, what is even more confusing, recommendations such as Fagan's, predicated upon a rejection of facile blueprint solutions, would themselves be regarded as a kind of blueprint. For example, many people in South Africa with whom I personally discussed the sobriety of the Fagan Report over the years, instantly drew the conclusion that I was recommending a 'return to 1948', which was impossible. By this they meant that the

* In 1973, when I lectured at the University of the Witwatersrand, not a single student in the class had ever even heard of the Fagan Commission.

creation of potentially independent Black homelands, one crucial premise of which it is true Fagan opposed, had rendered the Fagan Report obsolete. But Fagan had criticized the homeland idea as a basis for depriving Blacks of their legitimate rights in the towns; and we may confidently predict that the practical future in South Africa will see not simply the restoration of rights which were eliminated by the Nationalists in the 1950s and 1960s but the acquisition of rights which had never heretofore been possessed. More than this, however, Fagan as a conservative democrat had a principled opposition, like Ben Marais, to the elimination of any vested right of a group which it was not abusing (as distinguished from adding rights which public opinion is not prepared to accept). On this basis he opposed the dismantling on the part of the Nationalists of the 1936 settlement as well as the removal of the Coloureds in the Cape from the common roll.[2] But on this very basis he would, if he were alive today, oppose any tampering with the structure of homeland leadership that has been created under this regime. He in fact, we may recall, envisaged in 1963 bi-partisan consultation with these leaders along the same lines as that with the representatives of the Coloureds, Indians, and urban Blacks. If a functioning right or political institution is accepted as legitimate by public opinion, it should not be disturbed, however easily it can be seen as an anomaly by 'speculators'.[3] Fagan would therefore have been the first to say that anyone who, having read his Report, then concluded that one should take a broom and make a 'clean sweep' had completely misunderstood the essence of his politics. He would say that these 'speculators' had misunderstood the nature of decent politics; which is the concern with what is the best possible *now*. This concern presumes an awareness of the destructive effect of utopian solutions that ride roughshod over all the misery and wretchedness they cause in the short run, in which human lives are lived.

Altogether what is at issue here is not a 'return to the Fagan Report', as a kind of magic answer as to what to do now. It is rather an appreciation of Fagan as a model of how to think about race relations or constitutional politics generally, not just in 1948 or 1977, or even in South Africa, but always. It thus may not seem surprising if I say that it is not necessary for politicians to chain themselves to a desk and ponder the words of this Report, night and day, before they can act intelligently. In fact, since they will not do it anyway, it is not necessary that they read the Report at all. When they make sense, they will conform to the spirit of the Report whether they are aware of it or not. The guidance which Fagan can give in defending this common sense against its enemies, however, is another matter. The indications that I have given thus far and will now give in the sequel might usefully direct readers to the originals.

We come then to the eternal question of all decent politics, namely, what Fagan stated in the above letter about finding 'the best way of adapting ourselves to what is possible'. For Fagan this meant, of course, the best possible. But the best possible is imperceptible without guidance by some notion of the absolute best. For Fagan this was constitutional democratic government, which, as we shall see, he was content to define as government by consent. Now Fagan was not a theoretical man but a practical man. His published political writings consist of the Report of the Commission of which he was the chairman, and two tiny books, one of which is a set of extracts from public addresses. In the short preface to *Our Responsibility* he states that the book was originally written in Afrikaans. He then mentions that though bearing the surname and also the Christian names of an Irish ancestor (which is atypical for Afrikaners), he grew up in an Afrikaans-speaking home and was an Elder of the Dutch Reformed Church, to which he has retained his allegiance. He leaves no doubt whatsoever as to why he says this:

These facts are mentioned to explain the angle of approach which characterizes [this] book: it is that of an Afrikaner addressing himself to his fellow-Afrikaners.[4]

Whatever implications there are in Fagan's thought about the nature of democracy and of the political problem in South Africa must thus be related to this context. There is, to begin with, no attempt on his part to embark upon a theoretical, in the sense of detached, treatment of the race problem. Such a treatment could hardly avoid making light of certain prejudices and fears, the legitimacy of which Fagan assumed as an absolute base-line of any effective political education. This is the meaning of his presenting himself to the Afrikaners as an Afrikaner. His rhetoric thus took for granted—and as I noted in Chapter I he was quite explicit about this—the fact that his addressees understandably conceived of themselves as being in a terrible dilemma. On the one hand they saw no alternative to constitutional democracy in the modern world as the standard of the best regime. Even the pie-in-the-sky utopia fully conceded this. In this respect Fagan's pedagogical objective was of lesser magnitude than that of Abraham Lincoln who saw his country faced by the danger of a corruption of public opinion consisting of a rejection of equality.[5] On the other hand Fagan's addressees were afraid that the implementation of the demands of equality for the universalization of the franchise would lead to a political convulsion or, most simply, political suicide. The fear that this was unavoidable underlay the utopian solution. And as we noted in Chapter I Fagan clearly saw that the fiction in the utopia unavoidably and unnecessarily created injustice.

Fagan's objective was nothing other than the liberation from this dilemma of the minds of his addressees, who had the say in South Africa. In this respect he was at one with all thoughtful people in South Africa. Now Fagan fully conceded the legitimacy of the White fear about the extension of the franchise. We quoted earlier his statement that it would be like opening a flood-gate. Not only did he thus respect this fear. He agreed with it. But whether or not he privately shared it to quite the same intensity is really unimportant. What was decisive was his understanding that in a democracy a universal feeling cannot be ignored.[6] This is true, not only for the obvious political reasons, but for moral reasons as well. If democracy means government by consent of the governed, the expansion of its scope to preserve the constitutional regime, which is the heart of the matter in South Africa, cannot begin by nullifying the very principle which is the basis of this expansion. And in the concrete case, Fagan did not think that a people are 'racist' or immoral for being apprehensive about self-preservation. Since every person, indeed every ten-year-old child of normal intelligence, would agree that there is nothing immoral about not wanting to commit suicide, then everyone except a moron or a hypocrite would be a racist by this definition. Along these very lines Fagan would have categorically rejected the view that democracy obliges societies to commit themselves to courses of action regardless of whether people think they will lead to chaos.

On this score Fagan deviated from those liberals in South Africa who sought to shame the electorate for being unwilling to take risks. Now we must look once again at where he deviated just as fundamentally from the segregationists. In fact Fagan was in certain respects much closer to the liberals than he was to the segregationists, but for the most paradoxical of all reasons. This is that the former were much less overpowered than were the latter by a doctrinaire understanding of liberal democracy as a kind of tribunal. We must recall Fagan's critique of Stallard discussed earlier, which could be applied *a fortiori* to Dr. Verwoerd.[7] From Fagan's point of view both of them were obsessed with the general franchise as a norm which could permit of no practical modification. But, even in the 1930s, Dr. Brookes had seen the need for liberalism in South Africa to have a due respect for the normality of national (or ethnic) sentiments.[8] Prof. Hoernle also, in 1939, had challenged South Africans to 'think out afresh the meaning of liberal principles in application to a multi-racial situation'.[9] Mrs. Ballinger sums up this flexibility in liberal opinion very well:

Even before the change of government in 1948, it was becoming clear that a good deal of new political thinking would have to be done to produce a pattern to suit South African needs, that the old Cape liberal slogan of equal rights for all civilized men, inherited from Rhodes and conceived in the spirit of nineteenth century optimism, although still a good answer, was not going to be the whole answer to the problems of our multi-racial society in the twentieth century.[10]

After 1948, however, liberalism in South Africa was to be pushed into a defensive corner by the polemical confrontation, projected by the Nationalists themselves, between 'nationalism' and 'liberalism'. Note this 1948 statement of a leading Nationalist, Dr. N. J. Diederichs:

We are not concerned here with a fight between two ordinary political parties or organizations, or between two alternative governments . . . what is at issue is two outlooks on life, fundamentally so divergent that a compromise is entirely unthinkable. . . . It is a fight between nationalism on the one hand and liberalism on the other. . . . On the one hand, we have nationalism which believes in the existence, in the necessary existence, of distinct peoples, distinct languages, nations, and cultures, and which regards the fact of the existence of these peoples and cultures as the basis of its conduct. On the other hand we have liberalism, and the basis of its political struggle is the individual with his so-called rights and liberties. . . . Nationalism is the standpoint of members on this side of the House; and we say this ideal of liberalism is unnatural and impossible, and should it be achieved one day, which fortunately is not possible, the whole world would be poorer for it.[11]

Against this rhetorical onslaught, liberalism, on the defensive, became a carrier, not only of moral indignation, but also of a modicum of ill-concealed anti-Afrikaner racialism as well. In arguing against the impracticability of total territorial segregation, presented by the Nationalists as an expression of the most profound longing of 'Afrikaner nationalism', and also against the unequal laws the Nationalists put into practice, the English-speaking—and also Afrikaans-speaking—liberals were pushed into extremes where their flexibility did not disappear but certainly retreated below the surface of their public stance.

Fagan sought to preserve precisely the flexibility pointed to by Mrs. Ballinger. He also sought to disconnect it from anti-Afrikaner passions and bigotry. This is the sum and substance of his politics. As a politician, he saw very clearly that the Afrikaners were the decisive political group in South Africa. They had the power. All depended upon how they would use it. Either they would be led by doctrinaires, pandering to fear and bigotry while invoking the right of national self-preservation, or else they would be led by people like him. Part of his rhetoric in talking to his fellow-Afrikaners was thus to point out to them that the doctrinaire idea of apartheid, in the sense of total territorial segregation, was English in origin. He explicitly commented upon Shepstone and Stallard, but he could have also mentioned Creswell and Nicholls as well. He said this all very delicately since he would never stoop to anti-English or any other kind of demagogy. And he never regarded either these men or the Nationalist theorists as motivated by malice.[12] The rhetorical point he was making was very clear indeed. This is that the Afrikaners, left to themselves, had a native fund of practical common sense and practical decency. But they had one weakness. This is that, as a simple rural people, they were seducible by articulate foreigners, advancing their ideas about territorial segregation with the arrogance of imperial conquerors. He implicitly suggested that Hertzog, the so-called arch-segregationist, was so seduced.[13] There is, to be sure, a certain rhetorical exaggeration and oversimplification in this self-image he was projecting of pristine Afrikaner common sense. The debate between Reitz and Shepstone was by no means as one-sided as Fagan makes it out to be in his silence about Shepstone's position.[14] But, none the less, there is more than an atom of truth in this, given the power of the imperial factor in the aftermath of the South African War. And, in any event, we can see what he was trying to do politically. He knew, of course, that by the time Afrikaner nationalism had embraced all the views of Stallard, any political leadership to remind Afrikaners of what they really were or could rise to, in the light of their own history, would have to come from a fellow-Afrikaner. Only an Afrikaner could condemn as the purest bunk the notion that had been swallowed whole by both English and Afrikaner nationalist historians, namely, that Afrikaner history was the 'evolution of the apartheid idea'. This helps to explain why he did not ally himself with those English-speaking liberals in Johannesburg who welcomed and correctly understood the Fagan Report.[15] For the same reasons which Dr. Malherbe had pointed out in his letter to Smuts, about the impossibility of including Hofmeyr in a centre coalition, too close a political alliance with these non-Afrikaner liberals would have impaired his attempt to disconnect doctrinairism about the race problem from the *verkramptheid* regnant in the National Party. Without intimate knowledge of what Fagan's political calculations were, it is tempting to say that his decision to merge his National Union with the United Party was a blunder. Afrikaner nationalism at that point had to be faced by a different kind of Afrikaner voice, to offer a magnet and a refuge to those moderate Afrikaners who could neither stomach the *verkramptheid* of the National Party, nor what they regarded, rightly or wrongly, as the anti-Afrikaner atmosphere of the liberal groups. A tiny little party, with perhaps one or two members of parliament, but which kept alive common sense, might have served South Africa much better than the dilution of this practical impulse by the counter blueprints of the official Opposition. What would have happened to the United Party? The English-speaking liberals would have hived off as they did, with the converted preaching to the converted, leaving the rump of the old Dominion Party Natalians and *Bloedsappe*. Since moderate Afrikaners regarded this combination as a fossil, it would have been much easier to attract them from a truly independent position, where one could praise the Nationalists when they made sense and criticize them when they became tied up in doctrinaire knots. This would have precipitated a political vehicle for an opposition that was not 'counter-rhetorical', and was beyond the charge of disloyalty to Afrikanerdom. But this is admittedly said with benefit of hindsight. What is clear now is that the emergence of such an opposition still remains a political need for South Africa.

Fagan, then, facing his fellow-Afrikaners, saw them seduced by an impractical utopia not because of their rejection but because of their implicit acceptance of what they thought the premises of constitutional democracy demanded. They were in a dilemma only because they had been overpowered by rhetoric into thinking that the latter demanded the general franchise now or certainly in the immediate future. Thus there seemed to be a categorical choice between this or self-preservation. What Fagan did was to re-open the question of what constitutional democracy really demanded in South Africa, in a truly practical way. Where does one begin *now*? How does one begin *now*? In thinking through these questions with an absolute fidelity to the practical perspective, Fagan was led to a theoretical understanding of democracy that protected this most elemental aspect of all decent practice. The academics, liberal and nationalist, all talked about the need for new theory. But this is precisely what Fagan produced. And the amazing thing is that his theoretical grasp, of what comes down to the narrowness of a legalist or institutionalist understanding of democracy (for example, legal positivism), was presented primarily as indications within popular addresses. He avoided in his writing all those abstract questions which the race problem characteristically invites: is it 'soluble', what are its causes, is homogeneity better than heterogeneity, can nationalist aspirations ever really be prevented from disrupting a heterogeneous body politic, is total equality possible under any circumstances? He avoided them as *contentious speculations* about a future that now lies beyond our ken'.[16] The inflammation of public opinion by an obsession with these questions would only divert practice from the *agenda* or necessities of the situation. The nearest he comes to what might appear to be a 'general' thesis about the race problem is in the Report of the Fagan Commission itself, which is, understandably, somewhat drier in tone than his political writings proper. In the Report he stated the following:

Providence has ordained that White and Black shall dwell in South Africa side by side. Conflicts there may be—perhaps less in number if there could have been total territorial division, but then their intensity might have been greater and the results much more serious, as we have seen in Europe in the case of territorially separated nations that differ much less from each other than European and Bantu in South Africa. . . . We have simply to take up the task as it is laid upon us; *constant adaptation to changing conditions, constant regulation of contacts and smoothing out of difficulties between the races, so that all may make their contribution and combine their energies for the progress of South Africa.*[17]

Fagan thus avoided both a preoccupation with what Tocqueville called 'general ideas', by way of a lapse into academicism, and also the opposite vice. This is demagogic hysteria invoking these 'general ideas', or moralistic self-righteousness about serious grievances that he did not hesitate to mention. Altogether he preserved an absolutely correct proportion between principle and opinion in his practical role as a democratic educator. Though he never dropped the posture of speaking as an Afrikaner, his second book was published immediately in English (that is, for all South Africans). The situation by then—1963—had become much more grave.

Let us now follow along exactly how he thought out the problem of modern democracy. As will be evident his inquiry divided itself into a clarification of three questions. The first is what democracy is not. The second is what it is. The third is how it could take root 'in our difficult and seemingly intractable soil'.

Fagan tells, in an autobiographical account of the development of his thought, how he read Bryce's *Modern Democracies* about five or six years after it was first published in 1921, which 'set [him] thinking very hard'. Up to that point he had accepted as axiomatic and 'without any serious thought' the prevalent idea of democracy in the Western world as normal, ideal, and, indeed, 'the one truly correct form of government'. The reading of Bryce's book, as he admits, jarred him out of a certain complacency about his political assumptions. Bryce had opened his inquiry with a conventional definition of democracy as 'that form of government in which the ruling power of the state is vested in the members of the community as a whole'. This meant rule by the majority, since no other method has been found for determining the will of a community. But Bryce himself, in Fagan's account, immediately became aware of certain problems. The first was the dubious quality of regimes where more or less democratic institutions had been planted 'in a soil not prepared for them either by education in political principles or by the habits of constitutional government'. Military autocracies, not to mention plebiscitarian dictatorships, could arise in countries which on paper had democratic constitutions. On this basis Bryce cut out the whole array of Latin American republics as military dictatorships.[18]

The second problem noted by Bryce was the rarity of self-governing regimes in history prior to the modern theory of natural rights. During this pre-modern period the object of popular risings had been not self-government but good government. Fagan admitted that there was nothing new in these facts, either to him or to most of his readers. But suddenly, as is often the case with familiar facts, he saw them in a new light:

I said to myself: 'If democracy, in the sense of majority rule determined by a counting of heads, is the grand thing which I, and apparently everybody around me, believe it to be, how did mankind manage for thousands of years without it? And why in the world of today, with its praises being sung so loudly, is it making so little headway? Why has it often had to retreat in territories where at one time it appeared to have made a victorious advance? Why are so many states merely cashing in on the popularity of the word by applying it in name but not in fact?
These questions led unavoidably to the fundamental one:
In the conditions in which most communities exist, is democracy—defined in the words I have used above—not fitted to perform the functions required of a government, and can it fulfil that task only in exceptionally favourable conditions?[19]

Fagan states that he was shocked to find himself unable to give 'any but an affirmative answer' to this question. Yet a return to an acceptance of autocracy, however much more efficient it may be for managing the affairs of many countries, would be setting back the clock. He then

turned from Bryce's definition to the famous one of Abraham Lincoln:
'Government of the people, by the people, for the people.'

Does that mean the same as majority rule determined by a counting of heads?
I do not believe that it does.
It is much more general, much wider, much more elastic.
It does not prescribe a formula but enunciates a principle.
To me it is the spirit that matters, not the letter.
And I believe that the principle embodied in Lincoln's words can be
applied in various ways, differing according to the circumstances which call
for its application.[20]

The last sentence, recalling not only the words of Bryce but the
standpoint of all those thinkers—Burke, Tocqueville, Montesquieu,
Taine, and Rousseau himself—who sought to restore the importance
of circumstances, habits, and civic education, and to resist modern
natural-rights doctrinairism, might seem at first sight to be no more
than the voice of prudential common sense. To be sure this alone is not
trivial, given the power of such doctrinairism in the modern world.
But there was more to the matter than just this. Fagan, *incredibile dictu*,
saw in South Africa a 'wonderful field' for studying conditions that
were unique in the world, but which yet had aspects that might 'set
an example' of a system of government that would have 'the best
attributes of democracy'.[21] To be able to perceive the pedagogical
aspect of what was the potential resolution of the South African
problem, Fagan had to confront in a critical way the assumptions
constituting the current self-understanding of representative democracy in the successful cases. This is because the very success of the
successful democracies may have made them oblivious to the true
causes of their success and led them to identify the means with the end.
This error in self-understanding was bound, sooner or later, to injure
practice in the successful cases. It could not avoid—as Tocqueville
and Taine noted over a century ago—resulting in immediate convul-
sions as soon as people became deluded into thinking that they could
'make the world safe for democracy' by exporting what was in fact a
means—namely, the legal-institutional framework of the successful
democracies—to countries where circumstances made it impossible
for this means to subserve its true end.[22] Modern doctrinairism, of
course, is the refusal to face this problem. But Fagan did face it, which
indicates the depth of his intellectual venture.

What was the error at work in what had become the conventionalized
democratic theory in the successful democracies? Let us call it the
notion of a democratic system as a 'power-pie'. All men are by nature

equal and enemies to each other. Hence, the function of the political process is to guarantee equality of political power in and by its political institutions. Each and every individual must be equally 'represented' in the government. The constriction of the end of representative democracy to this 'power-equalizing' function dominated the concerns, certainly of American political science, from about 1900 until World War II. Corruption at the ballot box level by machine-politicians, over- and under-representation of constituencies, lobbies, and pressure groups—these were the topics that naturally came to the fore on consideration of the premise that the common good of a political democracy is exhaustively summed up by 'power-equalization' of each and every individual. It is no accident that a political science with this vitiated understanding of the common good became superseded by a 'new' and more 'realistic' political science, which frankly accepted the normality of 'élites' and the view that the end of 'power-equalization' was just a myth. The 'power-pie' became replaced by the 'power-game' as the subject of inquiry. It is no accident, also, that this 'new' political science became the object of a revolt in the late 1960s by a 'newer' political science, which demanded what may seem at first sight to be a return to the norm of the 'old' political science, of power-equalization. It is easy to see that both the 'new' and the 'newer' political science deviate more from what was actual practice in well-functioning demo- cracies than did the 'old' political science. This is so by virtue of the fact that the former *explicitly* jettisoned the possibility of rational discussion about the common good. We need not concern ourselves further with this point because Fagan, who was in this respect some- what 'old-fashioned', was not really confronted intellectually by the post-war developments in American political science. The problem for Fagan was still with the 'old' political science, namely, the inability of legalism to apprehend the problem of the tyranny of the majority, that is, a majoritarianism which effected its will strictly within the letter of the law:

Even where there is universal suffrage—'one man, one vote'—there are minorities that are outvoted and are unable to thwart the will of the majority. . . . The vote does not help them. Their only hope—and the only hope of appeasing them—lies in full opportunity to make their voices heard. They should feel that their views and their grievances are receiving attention, and that they can play a part in moulding the public opinion by which elections are swayed.[23]

In small democracies, with the greatest degree of homogeneity and social solidarity, where men were formed in common by the most pervasive civic education, the unity of the whole would dissipate the problem of the tyranny of a part. In large representative democracies, with distinct ethnic and class interests, the subordination of the interests of the whole to those of the larger part must always remain a potential problem. In South Africa, the fear that the institution of the general franchise would bring about such a situation was on the top of its politics. As we noted in Chapter I, Fagan saw that any 'tinkering' with the franchise would be regarded by the Whites as a 'concession', which would be the start of an irreversible slide towards one man, one vote.[24] It is equally true, however, that any such 'tinkering' short of the general franchise would be regarded by the non-Whites themselves as a sham. The qualified franchise, for example, raised the age-old question of who is qualifying whom, which is a political, not a legal question. Fagan, as we noted, saw the prudence of leaving the 'hot potato' of the franchise alone. But as indicated above he did more than simply leave the political problem in suspension. In pushing forward beyond the conventional notion of representation as a 'piece' of the 'power-pie', he saw the opening which could bring about the resolution of the political problem.

Fagan states that he was struck by a statement of Lord Fraser of Lonsdale, distinguishing between government by consent and government by representation:

I admire Dr. Verwoerd's ability as a party leader, but now that he has won the referendum it is surely the right time to approach government by consent even though government by representation is not in my opinion practical politics in South Africa. By the words government by consent I mean consultation with the Coloured people and the Natives in the urban areas that as far as possible takes account of their feelings and carries them along with you instead of forcing them into separate camps which inevitably breed resentment and ultimately rebellion.[25]

What struck Fagan in this comment was the fact that the terms 'government by consent' and 'government by representation', which usually are regarded as synonymous, were not regarded as synonymous or inseparable. This distinction confirmed Fagan in his judgement that facilities for full and effective discussion were the most essential element in democracy—'more essential, to my mind, than the vote'.[26] And there is every reason to believe that he had come to this judgement long before he had heard Lord Fraser's statement.

I will not repeat Fagan's practical recommendations, mentioned in Chapter I, about effective consultation with the non-Whites—now!— at all levels of government.[27] What is of interest here is the theoretical underpinning of that argument which could see the possibility of this without the general franchise. Fagan, after all, collided with the central notion of the conventional view that where there is legal inequality—in the concrete case, about the franchise—there will be inequality of power. And where there is inequality of power, the powerful will oppress or certainly ignore the weak, unless it serves their interests to do otherwise. Looking at South Africa, it would be easy to substantiate this proposition. Fagan himself noted how the three Native Representatives were simply brushed aside 'as a nuisance, at worst as a band of agitators', from the moment the Nationalists took power.[28] *But this derangement was, of course, essentially linked to the pursuit by the Government of an impossible policy to which no non-White or his Representative could conceivably agree.*

The heart of Fagan's analysis of modern democracy is his grasp of the dual function of parliament. And what he has to say about this is as applicable to homogeneous societies as it is to heterogeneous ones. South Africa's uniqueness thus turns out to be only the prod towards the perception of a broader ground of principle, under which its uniqueness can be subsumed and dealt with in a practical way. Its uniqueness thus ceases to terrorize the political imagination with expectations of an apocalypse.

He summed up this dual function of parliament as follows:

(1) It is the most conspicuous forum for a public discussion of political issues, and
(2) it finalizes these issues by voting on them.[29]

As he had made clear in the argument leading up to these sentences, the former was of greater importance. Obviously, in a parliamentary system, with the imposition of party discipline, a vote on party lines is a foregone conclusion. What counts is what is said. In this respect the function of an opposition is to keep on talking so as to influence the electorate. But this function in turn depends upon the existence of a press which publishes the discussions 'for all to read'.

It is the discussions, not the voting, that keep the electorate informed of the political issues on which they, at election time, have to give the ultimate decisions.[30]

As Fagan noted, modern dictators like the franchise. They simply abolish the opposition and a free press.[31]

Now all of Fagan's recommendations about effective consultation come down, in a nutshell, to integrating this process with the first and major function of parliament. The Whites had the vote. The non-Whites had no press of their own worth speaking of to inform White opinion of their views. It was for this reason that Fagan thought that the key to unblocking the log-jam was not simply bi-partisan consultation but coverage of and intelligent commentary about these deliberations in the press. Obviously the old saw can be reiterated, that where there is inequality of power, the weaker may be ignored. And, indeed, there is simply no institutional solution of this problem, in South Africa or anywhere else. If the Swiss Germans, who constitute 70% of the Swiss population, decided, in some flight of madness, to extirpate the other languages in the country at the price of a hideous civil war, one supposes that they could certainly start it. If they do not choose to do this, it is not because they are restrained by 'institutional' checks and balances or devices for 'sharing power'. It is because they believe it is wrong. A standard of right has taken hold which is a true restraint upon mere power. By the same token Fagan thought a start, indeed a new beginning that had never been made before in South Africa, could be made along these lines, in creating an atmosphere of goodwill, mutual trust, and common loyalty. This would be the effect of his policy, which did not necessitate a prior legalistic solution for 'power-sharing' via, perhaps, some fundamental national convention to 'wipe the slate clean'.

Fagan never deviated from his conviction that constitutional democracy in South Africa was incompatible with the institution of the general franchise or what is called all too glibly today 'majority rule'. But he was not a doctrinaire. He meant *now*, under *present* circumstances. If circumstances changed so that the general franchise was no longer feared as something that would wreck the constitutional regime, constitutional change towards the mode of representation in homogeneous constitutional regimes could and would take place with the consent of the governed. At the same time, so long as the deviations from the norm of the general franchise were seen as exceptions required *now* by the special circumstances of South Africa, there was no danger of their becoming a pretext for a caste system. Understood as exceptions, public opinion would not become corrupted by a misguided view of what the best or 'non-exceptional' was. This is the point which the majority Report of the Theron Commissioners restored for South Africa.

Fagan explicitly stated that in the new atmosphere created by the implementation of his policy machinery would be arising by which the ruling group—which in South Africa meant the Whites—

can keep its fingers on the pulse of all sections of the population, and so be in the most favourable position to know when the time is propitious, the common loyalty strong enough, for carrying the consultations beyond the range of matters of administration and considering the safety and feasibility of constitutional changes in the direction of a sharing of control at the highest level.[32]

He left it at that. But we must note in this statement the absence of the slightest trace of the view that one must (or must not) make guilt-ridden 'concessions' to stave off the day when the dyke would finally burst. As I said in Chapter I, Fagan explicitly repudiated the notion that a sound policy consists of 'making concessions'. Let me now cite his statement about this in full:

When I urge the necessity of a revision of our urban Bantu laws, I am often asked, 'What concessions are you prepared to make?'
My answer always is: 'I was not thinking of concessions.'
Then I am met with a blank stare, which clearly means to tell me that I am speaking in meaningless contradictions.
But I dislike the word 'concessions'.
It suggests a wrong approach.
As a judge on the bench I was under no duty to make concessions to litigants.
But I had to listen to them and do what was fair and just to them.
The suggestions I make in this book are intended to build up the best machinery and create the best atmosphere for ensuring good government.
Where there are groups with conflicting sentiments and interests, good government may often require concessions by one to another.
But that should be incidental.
It is not what I have in mind as the main object of group discussions.
And I believe that a genuine striving for good government is a better placatory policy than a bargaining about concessions.[33]

Having rejected for South Africa majority rule by the counting of heads, Fagan would have categorically denied that his policy was a 'concession' to its demands, a politically squeamish 'halfway house' that would put South Africa on a 'slippery slope' towards this eventuality. Yet this was the way Dr. Verwoerd construed the Fagan Report. And, to tell the truth, this is the way I myself saw it not only when I first read it but for several years after in the rhetorically permeated atmosphere of South African politics. This was because I had confused Fagan's policy with the franchise proposals of the United Party. These really were a 'halfway house' and were regarded as such by public opinion in South Africa, both White and Black. It was not until I had read his books and had understood, in his critique of plebiscitarianism, his principled argument about the demands of constitutionality, that I fully realized what his policy was. It was then that I saw the fundamental reason why he could deny that his policy was a 'concession' to a convulsive and tyrannical form of majority rule. This was (and is) that the implementation of his proposals *would* be an actualization of 'majority rule', albeit a politically sane and whole-some form, that would be admirably suited to the circumstances of South Africa. All the groups would have a voice in a government ruling by consent of the governed. They would feel it and know it. Uncluttered by sham institutional devices for 'sharing power', their consultations would be free of the urge to set these sham devices aside, in a divisive struggle for power that would set the groups at each other's throats. They would have every inclination to discuss rather than scream ultimata at each other, which the addressees would regard as an invitation to commit suicide. Discussion would take place, rather, within that framework of public reason which would protect, per-petuate, and perfect the constitutional quality of the regime, for the benefit of all. Fagan really sought to build a *tuiste vir die nageslag* (homeland for posterity),[34] but in a perspective which comprehended the *whole* of South Africa and *all* of its people.

Fagan's analysis raises a number of unanswered questions. Chief among these is whether the tendency towards doctrinairism, with its inanition of the common good, is inherent in modern democracy, and whether it is possible to deal with this problem theoretically without transcending its assumptions. Fagan, who was trying to broaden constitutional democracy in South Africa, did not touch this question. Indeed a practical man would well avoid doing so, given the alternative to constitutional democracy in the modern world. Within the horizons circumscribed by his goal, Fagan's essential concern was with the distinction between true and false democracy, the basis of democracy being a practically correct understanding of what is meant by 'the consent of the governed'. In the distinction between a voice and a vote what Fagan did was to liberate the meaning of 'consent of the governed' from its corruption by legal positivism. He could then look at the problem of modern democracy with a political or trans-legalistic standard of what a decent constitutional regime ought to be. With this standard of civic excellence, he could see that a society in which politicians had to argue their cases in the broad light of day, to persuade and gain adherents, was morally superior to one in which rulers arbitrarily imposed their will upon a mute public. At the same time he could defend political democracy against its transformation into that perversion of equality, namely, standardless majoritarianism, before which legal positivism was prepared to prostrate itself. The latter could not admit that a majority could be wrong, even a government which in the name of the majority 'legally' abandoned political freedom, a free press, and a constitutional opposition, while brazenly calling itself a 'one-party republic'. But Fagan, and I believe most men of common sense, could. Between these two poles Fagan, transcending the constrictions of legalism in his emphasis upon the 'spirit' of the regime, could grasp sight of the highest political consideration, namely, the conditions for the perpetuation of the constitutional regime. What may seem paradoxical at first sight, but is not really upon reflection, is that the principle of consent, understood in a wholly non-legalistic way, proves to be the key for initiating the practical reduction and, ultimately, disappearance of the racial oligarchy or the inequality between those who do and those who do not have the constitutional say. The Whites have to be persuaded that they were not in the process of committing suicide. The Blacks have effectively to be consulted for justice to be done. And the very implementation of the latter will *begin* to actualize the former. Fagan was not so simple-minded as to think that by effective consultation he meant that everyone should be satisfied, which would not occur, of course, under any conditions. He used, as we saw, the analogy of a judge on the bench, who does not try to satisfy the litigants but to do justice between them. This, as he stated, is all that the litigants can demand from him. 'And that is all that the various groups can demand from the consultations.' He then went on to say that if these groups made unreasonable and unacceptable proposals, and walked out on the talks when they failed to get their way, such conduct would be 'nothing new'.[35] What would be new, however, would be the future of such deliberations if they became openly discussed by the organs of a free public opinion. To the metaphor of the judge Fagan could add the metaphor of the jury, namely, public reason.

In sum, what Fagan sought to bring about in South Africa might be described as the missing part of Lincoln's career. This refers, of course, to what Lincoln, had he not been prematurely struck down, might have been able to accomplish towards a resolution of the race problem in the South after emancipation. The Blacks had to be transformed from 'freemen' into citizens. But how could this be done, in the face of the same kind of White fears, about being outnumbered by the people who were yesterday 'down there', that one finds in South Africa and many other countries, past and present? Lincoln, in fact, had proposed, shortly before his death, a qualified franchise for those

6

Blacks who were educated and who had fought in the Union army.[36] This might have got things started on a sound footing in a way which would not have invited a reaction. It might also work in South Africa at some time in the future. But no one can tell exactly when. The political success or possibility of such arrangements depends upon circumstances governing the content of public opinion. But then the task presents itself of finding the openings which exist now, as contrasted with waiting passively for the circumstances to change. Guiding one's understanding of this task is the awareness that citizenship in a democracy consists of more than mere legal equality or equality to scream the 'little catechism of natural rights'. It presupposes a common stake in the society, loyalty, habits, civic education, and experience of self-government by discussion. Booker T. Washington summed it up in the two leading maxims of his policy. The first was that the White man could keep the Black man in the ditch only by getting down there with him. The second was that no one really becomes a free citizen by virtue of a piece of paper.

Notes

Chapter I

1. Eric A. Walker, *A History of Southern Africa*, 3rd ed., Longman, London, 1964, 546.
2. D. W. Krüger, *South African Parties and Policies 1910–1960: A Select Source Book*, Human and Rousseau, Cape Town, 1960, 71.
3. Ibid., 29.
4. H. J. Simons and R. E. Simons, *Class and Colour in South Africa 1850–1950*, Penguin, Harmondsworth, 1969, 285.
5. Krüger, op. cit., 74.
6. Ibid., 73.
7. Ibid.
8. Ibid., 74.
9. Margaret Ballinger, *From Union to Apartheid: A Trek to Isolation*, Praeger, New York, and Bailey Bros, London, 1969, 58.
10. D. W. Krüger, *The Making of a Nation: A History of the Union of South Africa 1910–1961*, Macmillan, Johannesburg and London, 1969, 187.
11. H. A. Fagan, *Our Responsibility: A Discussion of South Africa's Racial Problems*, Die Universiteits-Uitgewers, Stellenbosch, 1960, 10; Ballinger, op. cit., 63.
12. Ballinger, op. cit., 146.
13. Walker, op. cit., 676.
14. Michael Roberts and A. E. G. Trollip, *The South African Opposition, 1939–1945*, Longmans, Green & Co., Cape Town, 1947.
15. Kenneth A. Heard, *General Elections in South Africa 1943–1970*, Oxford University Press, London, 1974, 27.
16. Krüger, *The Making of a Nation*, 223.
17. Ballinger, op. cit., 267.
18. Ibid.
19. Krüger, *The Making of a Nation*, 187; Heard, op. cit., 33.
20. Thomas Karis and Gwendolen M. Carter, eds., *From Protest to Challenge; A Documentary History of African Politics in South Africa 1882–1964*, vol. 2, Hoover Institution Press, Stanford, 1973, 238.
21. Ibid., 244.
22. Heard, op. cit., 33ff., 43ff.
23. Jean Van Der Poel, *Selections from the Smuts Papers*, vol. VII, Cambridge University Press, Cambridge, 1973, 237–45.
24. Ibid., 242f.

25. Ibid., 238.
26. Ibid., 241f.
27. Ibid., 244.
28. Ibid., 246. See also W. K. Hancock, *Smuts, The Fields of Force 1919–1950*, Cambridge University Press, Cambridge, 1968, 513–15, for a description of this episode.
29. Booker T. Washington, *Frederick Douglass* (excerpted in Howard Brotz, ed., *Negro Social and Political Thought 1850–1920: Representative Texts*, Basic Books, New York, 1966, 383).
30. See Malherbe's letter to Smuts in Van Der Poel, op. cit., 242.
31. Ibid.
32. E. G. Malherbe, *Education in South Africa*, vol. II, Juta & Co., Cape Town, 1976, 94.
33. Alexander Davis, *The Native Problem*, Chapman and Hall, London, 1903, 119.
34. *Report of the Transvaal Local Government [Stallard] Commission*, T.P. 1–1922, para. 42.
35. *Report of the Native Laws [Fagan] Commission 1946–1948*, U.G. No. 28–1948, para. 29 (cited subsequently as the Fagan Report).
36. Ibid.
37. H. A. Fagan, *Co-existence in South Africa*, Juta & Co., Cape Town, 1963, 20.
38. Ibid., 45.
39. Ibid.
40. Fagan, *Our Responsibility*, 66.
41. Ibid.
42. Fagan, *Co-existence in South Africa*, 110.
43. Fagan, *Our Responsibility*, 66.
44. Fagan, *Co-existence in South Africa*, 98.
45. Ibid., 23.
46. C. M. Tatz, *Shadow and Substance in South Africa; A Study in Land and Franchise Policies Affecting Africans 1910–1960*, University of Natal Press, Pietermaritzburg, 1962, 116.
47. Fagan, *Co-existence in South Africa*, 50.
48. Krüger, *South African Parties and Policies*, 402.
49. Ballinger, op. cit.; E. H. Brookes, *Apartheid: A Documentary Study of Modern South Africa*, Routledge and Kegan Paul, London, 1968; Gwendolen M. Carter, *The Politics of Inequality*, Thames and Hudson, London, 1958.
50. Carter, op. cit., 119–44.
51. A. N. Pelzer, ed., *Verwoerd Speaks: Speeches 1948–1966*, APB Publishers, Johannesburg, 1966, 12.
52. Fagan saw that Dr. Malan 'was adopting the old expedient of governments faced with a problem which they themselves do not know how to tackle. He appointed a commission.' Fagan, *Our Responsibility*, 28.
53. *Verwoerd Speaks*, 278, 'Speech Concerning the Bill Promoting Bantu Self-government', Senate, 20 May 1959.
54. Fagan, *Our Responsibility*, 49.
55. Heard points out that the percentage poll in this referendum was higher than in subsequent elections with the Bantu homelands policy providing the dominant issue. Heard, op. cit., 170.
56. *Verwoerd Speaks*, 13.

57. Ibid., 216–47.
58. Fagan, *Co-existence in South Africa*, 109.
59. *Die Transvaler*, 4 May 1938.
60. Edward Feit, *African Opposition in South Africa: The Failure of Passive Resistance*, Hoover Institution Press, Stanford, 1967.
61. Fagan, *Our Responsibility*, 69.
62. Edward Feit, *Urban Revolt in South Africa, 1960–1964*, Northwestern University Press, Evanston, 1971.
63. Heard, op. cit., 125–8.
64. Ben Marais, for example, in *The Two Faces of Africa*, Shuter and Shooter, Pietermaritzburg, 1964, 32, distinguished between apartheid as common-sense separate development and apartheid as an ideology of separation for the sake of separation, which legitimated the kind of racial discrimination that hurt people and created antagonisms. It was going to take the Government another ten years before it could say that its policy recognized the validity of precisely this distinction.
65. 'Press Digest' of the S.A. Jewish Board of Deputies, 20 June 1969.
66. Ibid.
67. J. H. P. Serfontein, *Die Verkrampte Aanslag*, Human and Rousseau, Cape Town, 1970, 241–6.
68. H. Lever, *The South African Voter: Some Aspects of Voting Behaviour*, Juta & Co., London, 1973.
69. See Howard Brotz, 'Theory and Practice: Ethnomethodology versus Humane Ethnography', *Jewish Journal of Sociology*, December 1974, 225–36.
70. *Die Segregasie Vraagstuck* (Address given by General Hertzog at Smithfield, 13 November 1925), Nasionale Pers, Cape Town, n.d., 14.
71. Yves R. Simon, *Philosophy of Democratic Government*, University of Chicago Press, 1951.
72. E. H. Brookes, *The Colour Problems of South Africa*, Kegan Paul, London, 1934, 53.

Chapter II

1. S. Herbert Frankel, 'The Tyranny of Economic Paternalism in Africa', *OPTIMA*, December 1960, Supplement, 3f.
2. Social and Economic Planning Council, *The Native Reserves and Their Place in the Economy of the Union of South Africa*, Report No. 9, U.G. No. 32–1946 (cited subsequently as the Van Eck Report), para. 21.
3. 'Native Policy: The Reitz-Shepstone Correspondence of 1891–1892', *Natalia*, Journal of the Natal Society, September 1972, 10–14.
4. Fagan, *Our Responsibility*, 15.
5. The Van Eck Report, paras. 21, 22.
6. Fagan, *Our Responsibility*, 16.
7. Ibid., 19ff.
8. Tatz, op. cit., 6.
9. *Report of the South African Native Affairs Commission, 1903–1905*, para. 207.
10. Ibid., para. 181.
11. Ibid., paras 193, 198.
12. Ibid., para. 443.

13. Ibid., paras 248, 249, 383.
14. Ibid., para. 357.
15. Ibid., para. 374.
16. Ibid., paras 374, 375.
17. Edgar H. Brookes, *The History of Native Policy in South Africa from 1830 to the Present Day*, J. L. Van Schaik, Pretoria, 1927, 135.
18. *Report of the South African Native Affairs Commission*, para. 144.
19. Ibid., paras 146, 147.
20. Ibid., para. 198.
21. Ibid., para. 192.
22. Margaret Creswell, *An Epoch in the Political History of South Africa in the Life of Frederic Hugh Page Creswell*, Balkema, Cape Town, 1956, 5.
23. Ibid., 33–7.
24. Ibid., 39.
25. A statement from the *Pall Mall Gazette* quoted in Davis op. cit., 126f. See also Lionel Phillips, *Transvaal Problems: Some Notes on Current Politics*, John Murray, London, 1905, 66, 255.
26. Supra, p. 34.
27. Supra, p. 27.
28. T. R. H. Davenport, 'African Townsmen? South African Urban Areas Legislation', *African Affairs*, April 1969, 95–109; *The Beginnings of Urban Segregation in South Africa: The Natives (Urban Areas) Act of 1923 and its Background*, Occasional Paper Number Fifteen, Institute of Social and Economic Research, Rhodes University, Grahamstown, 1971.
29. G. Heaton Nicholls, *South Africa in My Time*, Allen & Unwin, London, 1961, 277–93.
30. *House of Assembly Debates*, 4 May 1936, col. 2897; italics not in original.
31. W. H. Hutt, *The Economics of the Colour Bar*, André Deutsch, London, 1964, 78.
32. *Report of Native Economic Commission 1930–1932*, U.G. No. 22–1932, para. 500.
33. Ibid., paras 76–8, 95.
34. Ibid., paras 72–3.
35. Ibid., paras 103–6, 195.
36. Ibid., paras 344–6.
37. Ibid., para. 193.
38. Ibid., para. 191.
39. Ibid., paras 140–3.
40. Ibid., para. 174.
41. Ray Phillips, *The Bantu Are Coming: Phases of South Africa's Race Problem*, Student Christian Movement Press, London, 1930, 70.
42. *Report of Native Economic Commission*, paras 49, 179.
43. The Van Eck Report, para. 13.
44. Ibid., paras 184–8; the Fagan Report, para. 56.
45. The Van Eck Report, para. 53.
46. The Fagan Report, paras 41, 50–63.
47. This process was anticipated in Colin Clark, *The Conditions of Economic Progress*, 2nd edn., Macmillan, London, 1951.
48. See Maurice S. Evans, *Black and White in South East Africa: A Study in Sociology*, Longman, Green & Co., London, 1911, 161, for a description of the inefficiency of Black gang-labour.

49. Donald Dewey, 'Negro Employment in Southern Industry', *Journal of Political Economy*, August 1952, 279–93.
50. G. V. Doxey, *The Industrial Colour Bar in South Africa*, Oxford University Press, Cape Town, 1961.
51. Simons and Simons, op. cit., 335–9. Professor Houghton informed me that if the typographical union had held fast to the norm of the rate for the job, it would have wrecked the Black press.
52. Sheila T. L. Van der Horst, 'The Effects of Industrialisation on Race Relations in South Africa', in Guy Hunter, ed., *Industrialisation and Race Relations*, Oxford University Press, London, 1965, 118f.
53. D. Hobart Houghton, *The South African Economy*, 4th edn., Oxford University Press, Cape Town, 1976, 148. Houghton points out that this became reinforced by trade union pressure.
54. Doxey, op. cit., 15.
55. Hutt, op. cit., 96.
56. *Rand Daily Mail*, 4 October 1973.
57. Ibid.
58. *Report of the Commission of Inquiry into matters related to the Coloured Population Group*, R.P. 38–1976 (cited subsequently as the Theron Report), para. 178.
59. Ibid.
60. *Summary of the Report of the Commission for the Socio-Economic Development of the Bantu Areas within the Union of South Africa*, U.G. 61–1955, 138, para. 16.
61. *House of Assembly Debates*, 1 May 1975, col. 5233.
62. Paul N. Malherbe, *Multistan: A way out of the South African dilemma*, David Philip, Cape Town, 1974.
63. Frankel, op. cit.
64. Trevor Bell, *Industrial Decentralisation in South Africa*, Oxford University Press, Cape Town, 1973, 254–61.

Chapter III

1. *House of Assembly Debates*, 23 March 1939, col. 2232.
2. Ibid., col. 2233.
3. *Report of the Indian Penetration Commission*, U.G. No. 39–1941, para. 324.
4. 'My View of Segregation Laws', in Howard Brotz, ed., *Negro Social and Political Thought*, 461.
5. Fagan, *Our Responsibility*, 71.
6. Muriel Horrell, *Legislation and Race Relations*, South African Institute of Race Relations, Johannesburg, 1971, 35.
7. The Theron Report, para. 5.
8. Ibid., para. 4.
9. *House of Assembly Debates*, 1 May 1975, col. 5232.
10. Supra, p. 117.
11. The Fagan Report, paras 39–49.
12. Nathan Glazer and Daniel Patrick Moynihan, *Beyond the Melting Pot*, 2nd edn., M.I.T. Press, Cambridge, Mass., 1970.

13. Samuel Lubell, *The Future of American Politics*, 2nd edn. rev., Doubleday Anchor Books, Garden City, 137–43.
14. Glazer and Moynihan, op. cit. See also Leo Strauss's discussion of the Jewish problem in his preface to his *Spinoza's Critique of Religion*, Schocken Books, New York, 1965, 6f., where the insolubility of this problem in liberal society is not simply faced but faced in the light of any possible non-liberal alternatives in the modern world.
15. Philip Mayer, *Townsmen or Tribesmen: Conservatism and the Process of Urbanization in a South African City*, Oxford University Press, Cape Town, 1963; B. A. Pauw, *The Second Generation: A Study of the Family among Urbanized Bantu in East London*, Oxford University Press, Cape Town, 1963; Monica Wilson and Archie Mafeje, *Langa: A Study of Social Groups in an African Township*, Oxford University Press, Cape Town, 1963.
16. Bengt G. M. Sundkler, *Bantu Prophets in South Africa*, 2nd edn., Oxford University Press, London, 1961.
17. 'Black Society Makes the Scene', *News/Check*, 24 July 1970.
18. Krüger, *South African Parties and Policies*, 407.
19. The Theron Report, para. 94.
20. Ibid., para. 95.
21. Ibid., para. 153.
22. Leo Strauss, *The City and Man*, Rand McNally, Chicago, 1964, 19–21.
23. Ben Marais, in his *The Two Faces of Africa*, 32, pointed this out very clearly.
24. *House of Assembly Debates*, 3 June 1975, cols. 7228–78.
25. The Theron Report, para. 9.

Chapter IV

1. Fagan, *Our Responsibility*, 24f.
2. Ibid., 57.
3. T. B. Macaulay, *History of England*, vol. 2, Everyman's Library, London, 445f.
4. Fagan, *Our Responsibility*, preface.
5. Harry V. Jaffa, *Crisis of the House Divided*, Doubleday, Garden City, 1959.
6. Fagan, *Our Responsibility*, 61; Jaffa, op. cit., 376 (quoting Lincoln).
7. Supra, p. 27.
8. Brookes, *The Colour Problems of South Africa*, 21.
9. R. F. Alfred Hoernle, *Race and Reason*, Witwatersrand University Press, Johannesburg, 1945, 147.
10. Ballinger, op. cit., 397f.
11. *House of Assembly Debates*, 16–20 August 1948, col. 500.
12. Fagan, *Our Responsibility*, 35.
13. Ibid., 43. See also Rodney Davenport, 'The Triumph of Colonel Stallard', *South African Historical Journal*, vol. II, 1970, 77–96, for an account of Stallard's role in the introduction of influx control in 1937. Dr. Davenport points out that Hertzog did not think this would work. I might add that if an Afrikaner Nationalist had confronted Stallard in the 1920s with the thesis that Fagan was to articulate in the 1940s, namely, that the Westminster norm would have to be adapted to the circumstances of South Africa, he would probably have been suspected of wanting to 'cut the painter'.
14. Ibid., 12ff.

15. South African Institute of Race Relations, *A Survey of Race Relations 1947–48*, Johannesburg, 2.
16. Fagan, *Co-existence in South Africa*, 107.
17. The Fagan Report, para. 31.
18. Fagan, *Co-existence in South Africa*, 4ff.
19. Ibid., 9.
20. Ibid., 10.
21. Ibid.
22. Alexis de Tocqueville, *De La Démocratie en Amérique*, vol. 1, Gallimard, Paris, 1961, 321 (English translation by George Lawrence, Fontana Library, 1966, 379); H. Taine, *Notes sur l'Angleterre*, Hachette, Paris, 1919, 216f. (English translation by W. F. Rae, Strahan & Co., London, 1872, 197).
23. Fagan, *Co-existence in South Africa*, 47.
24. Supra, p. 27.
25. Fagan, *Co-existence in South Africa*, 25.
26. Ibid., 82.
27. Supra, p. 31.
28. Fagan, *Co-existence in South Africa*, 81.
29. Ibid., 82.
30. Ibid.
31. Ibid., 79.
32. Ibid., 75.
33. Ibid., 110.
34. This was a slogan of Purified Nationalism.
35. Fagan, *Co-existence in South Africa*, 119.
36. Jaffa, op. cit., 386.

Index